What the tennis world says about
Dick Myers and **Tennis for Humans:
Winning Hints, Tips, and Strategies
for the Competitive Club Level Player**

"Fast-paced…chock-full of great tips and insightful ideas…sure to improve your singles and doubles game."
—*David Dusek, Tennis magazine*

"I liked the concept, the approach, and the straightforward language. Dick Myers, as did Howard Cosell, tells it like it is."
—*Dick Squires, publisher of Tennis USTA*

"Dick has the ability to bring out the very best in a player. Dick should coach coaches on how to coach."
—*Deborah Gresty, Conde Nast Traveller, UK*

"A unique book…highly informative…with humor sprinkled throughout."
—*Buffalo News*

"A unique, informative, and funny instructional book."
—*Tennis Week*

"*Tennis for Humans* is remarkable and user friendly…steady and often immediate improvement can be expected."
—*Atlantic Racquet Press*

"This simple, reader-friendly book can help anyone who plays tennis."

—NSB Obsever

"A pragmatic outline for what really matters in tennis and a reminder for the experienced player of what to not waste time worrying about."

—Milena Volkova

"The in-depth information on each page will help athletes play smarter tennis with instant results."

—Independent Publisher's Group

"Dick's teaching style is very straightforward, humorous, and very effective. Tennis for Humans is all of these things and more. It will help anyone who plays tennis."

—Bob Callaway, author<br>and perhaps the world's oldest teaching pro

"Myers has served up a winner. Reading Tennis for Humans is as much fun as playing the game."

—Woody Schneider, Grand Central Racquet

"A more approachable book."

—ForeWord magazine

"Tennis for Humans is a grand slam winner!"

—Douglas Burack

"Tennis for Humans is the best tennis book since Gallwey's The Inner Game."

—Mike Adamson, BVI National Champion

"*Tennis for Humans* won't teach you the art of the deal, but it is one of the best investments you'll ever make to improve your tennis game."

–Donald Trump

"All players of all levels: Read *Tennis for Humans* by Dick Myers."

–Greg Moran, author of Beyond Big Shots

"Myers successfully adds a new spin to how-to books."

–Inside Tennis

"Contains dozens of hints, tips, and strategies to help you win."

–Florida Tennis

"Intriguing, bouncy, interesting. My review is simple: I recommend it to all."

–Joe Dinoffer, Coach Tennis America

"Dick Myers is a great teacher, a great player, and a good friend."

–Rich DeVos, Orlando Magic owner,<br>Amway founder

"Sections on practicing, shot selection and effective poaching are sure to improve your game."

–Court Time magazine

"Very simply *Tennis for Humans* makes sense. It is a fun and informative read."

–Anne Dobbs

# TENNIS

## FOR HUMANS

# TENNIS

## FOR HUMANS

### Winning Hints, Tips, and Strategies
for the
### Competitive Club Level Player

*Anniversary Edition*

RICHARD B. MYERS

TWO THOUSAND THREE ASSOCIATES
TTTA

Published by
**TWO THOUSAND THREE ASSOCIATES**
4180 Saxon Drive, New Smyrna Beach, Florida 32169
Phone: 386.427.7876  Fax: 386.423.7523

Printed in the United States of America

**Library of Congress Cataloging-in-Publication Data**
Myers, Richard B. (Richard Brooks), 1946-
    Tennis for humans: winning hints, tips, and strategies for the
    competitive club level player / Richard B. Myers
    p.   cm.
    Includes index.
    1. Tennis   I. Title
    GV995.M98   1997
    796.342'2--dc21           96-54275
                            CIP

ISBN-13: 9781892285133
ISBN-10: 1-892285134

10 9 8 7 6 5 4 3 2 1

*For*
*Samantha*

*from North Street*
*to Bourbon Street*
*to Wall Street*
*to South Baptist Street – still the best kid ever*

**ACKNOWLEDGMENTS**

Special thanks to Jon Corhern at Imagecraft Designs.

I would like to thank my wife, Pam, for her dedication to this project, for her talents and skills and patience, and for her immeasurable help. Without her there is no book.

# INTRODUCTION

*Tennis for Humans* will not help you beat players like Federer or the Williams sisters. It is a simple book for regular players. The hope is you will use the book to enjoy tennis more and win more often.

The book, like the game of tennis, is supposed to be fun. The goals in the book are serious, but hopefully the book will make you smile occasionally when you're reading it; and smile often when you are walking off the tennis court after another victory.

There is an easy flow to the book, a loose continuity. The information, and the hints, reminders, ideas, and concepts are offered in small, accessible portions throughout the book.

The information is sometimes repetitive and sometimes overlapping. It often says the same thing in different ways in several different places. It does so on purpose – because people hear, see, and learn differently, and repetition is often an effective way to help people learn.

*Tennis for Humans* contains individual case studies and generalizations and oversimplifications and some seeming contradictions. Tennis is an art, not a science. A suggestion that successfully raises your game to a new level might do much less for another player.

The suggestions in this book work. They can make a huge difference in your effectiveness as a tennis player. I have seen many different humans become better, more effective tennis players by trying and using these suggestions. I have seen it happen with players of all levels and all ages for over four decades.

So, go ahead and experiment. Have some fun. Play better, smarter, more effective tennis.

*—R.B.M.*

# TABLE OF CONTENTS

## CHAPTER 1

# A FEW ANSWERS

*"Start where you are. Use what you have.*
*Do what you can."*
*– Arthur Ashe*

## WHO IS THIS BOOK FOR?

*Tennis for Humans* is for tennis players at varying levels of play, from the advanced beginner to the club champion. It is for players who would like to have more fun on the court and win more. And all of us, as Arthur Ashe's quote indicates, have to "start from where we are." And whether your goal is to win a USTA tournament, a club or town championship, a team match, or a one-setter for neighborhood bragging rights, the hope is this book will enable you to "use what you have" better and "do what you can" smarter.

# WHY IS IT CALLED *TENNIS FOR HUMANS*?

The term "humans" is used playfully to differentiate the vast numbers of club-level players from the tournament players and teaching pros who make their living on a tennis court, and the "superhuman" professionals we watch on television. If you don't receive a check when you leave the court, then you're probably a tennis-playing human.

Realistically, not many "humans" will ever consistently hit a backhand down the line like Rafael Nadal or return serve as effectively as Roger Federer or serve like Serena Williams. No matter how many articles or books you read or lessons you take, you will not be playing at that level. But that doesn't mean you can't improve and become a smarter player, give away fewer points, and win more of those close matches.

# CAN THIS BOOK REALLY MAKE ME A BETTER PLAYER?

Unquestionably, yes. If you read through this book and employ even a few of the simple suggestions, you will be a more effective player . . . almost immediately in some cases. You will be making fewer errors, forcing more errors from your opponent, and controlling what happens on the court. And if you are controlling what happens on the court, you'll be playing better tennis and winning more often.

# GET REAL. DOESN'T IT TAKE YEARS OF PRACTICE AND HARD WORK TO REALLY GET BETTER?

The surprising answer is no! The majority of players who have been playing and practicing for years remain at the same level because they make the same mental mistakes, are unclear of their goals on the court, and misunderstand their own strengths and weaknesses.

Many players are making tennis a much harder game than it actually is. In fact, the very things they are trying to do to win are actually causing them to lose. They are trying to execute difficult shots beyond their skill level when simpler, smarter shots would work.

Players who have been at the same level for years can raise that level significantly in a few weeks or months. And ironically, they will become better by using shots and concepts that are easier to employ than those they have been using or trying to use.

## HOW IS THIS BOOK ORGANIZED?

Loosely. The book is divided into 14 chapters with each one focusing on a different topic. And even if you don't play singles or mixed doubles, you should probably take a look at those chapters. Remember, the men's chapter isn't just for men, or the women's chapter just for women. All the chapters in the book are for all tennis players. The whole book is on tennis.

In between each chapter there are various features. These features simply offer another, different way of getting information across to you. Whether it is a "test" or a list of "nevers" or a " case study" or a "conversation with the coach," it is simply various hints, tips, and strategies to help you play smarter tennis.

## WHAT IF MY OPPONENT HAS READ THIS BOOK, TOO?

Hopefully you both will end up playing tennis on a higher level. The winner may be the one who was executing better on that particular day or it might be the player who used the ideas in this book most effectively.

# TENNIS FACT OR TENNIS FICTION?

### 1. Well-hit ground strokes clear the net by two or three inches.

FICTION: Especially for the club level player, one or two inches above the net is not a safe enough margin of error. Well-hit ground strokes should probably consistently clear the net by a foot or more.

### 2. The easiest time to "take the net" is by following in after your serve.

FICTION: Following your serve to net, especially in doubles, is a fine idea. But perhaps the easiest time to take the net is on return of your opponent's second serve. You have the advantage of being inside the baseline to execute the return, so you should be able to get into better position, closer to the net, to make the first volley.

### 3. All else being equal, the smarter player will usually win.

FACT: Obviously a very smart 3.5-level player will not usually beat a not so smart 4.5 player, but if the players have fairly equal skills and abilities, the smarter player will win more often.

### 4. If someone has been playing tennis for many years at the same level, that is "their level." They are not going to improve.

TOTAL FICTION: Not every player can improve from, let's say, a 3.5 to a 4.5. But every tennis player, repeat, every tennis player, can improve tremendously by playing smarter.

## CHAPTER 2

# HOW
# TO USE
# THIS BOOK

*"It is difficult*
*for most people to imagine*
*the creative process in tennis."*
*– Virginia Wade*

## USE IT

Just buying this book won't improve your tennis. In fact, just reading through this book will probably only improve your game slightly. But if you use the ideas in the book as a basis for "the creative process in tennis" that Virginia Wade is talking about, you will improve your game noticeably.

*Tennis for Humans* is a simple book. It isn't filled with mystical secrets or magical plans. Much of the information — the tennis hints and suggestions and reminders — is not new. Some of it you have heard for years. On the other hand, some of it is the **exact opposite** of what you have heard or thought for years.

Pay very close attention to both the simple stuff you have heard for years — the stuff you think you already know, and the stuff that is the opposite of what you have heard and thought for years — the stuff that you probably did not know that may surprise you.

Use the book to shake up and wake up your thinking about tennis. Use it to approach familiar problems from a new direction, to ask new questions, to experiment, and to have fun. Use it to make your brain the most effective weapon in your tennis arsenal.

## SKIP AROUND IN THE BOOK

The subtitle says it is "winning hints, tips, and strategies for the competitive club level player." Perhaps it should have been called an "anthology" for winning, or "a bunch of "stuff" to help you win. You can certainly read the book from front to back, but it is also meant to be glanced through and read piece by piece — a "question for the coach" today, a chapter tomorrow, a true/false test the next day. Pick it up and skim it until something catches your attention and then try to incorporate that "something" into your tennis game the next time you step on the court.

Keep the book on your bedside table; feature it in the smallest room in the house; or even toss it on a shelf in your tennis locker. Look at it before a practice or after a match or during a plane ride. You can systematically integrate the ideas into your game or randomly try several from time to time. The information and the messages are simple, and integrating them into your game is simple as well.

You will discover that you do not have to make drastic changes in your game to make a big difference in your effectiveness on the court. Some players might make four changes in their game in one match, others might perfect one small change in four matches. If you try to apply at least one "new" concept or idea from this book each time you play, you will get better. Guaranteed.

## BE REALISTIC

All of us would like to play like the "big boys and girls" on television — serving blistering aces, driving backhand winners down the line, executing exquisite drop shots with a surgeon's touch. But, realistically, regular humans are never going to be able to do these things as consistently as the pros.

Most regular humans won't even get close. Most likely, you don't have the talent, the coaching, the practice time, or the desire to devote that much time to your tennis. You'll have to "get better" with less talent and less time than the pros, with fewer coaches and fewer practice sessions.

You are going to have to get better by using your head, by beating your opponents with combinations of ordinary shots instead of those highlight–film wonders from the tube. You will have to become more effective by making fewer errors in executing your shots and by setting smart and realistic goals.

You may never play like the pros but that certainly doesn't mean you can't play better, smarter tennis. You will probably not start beating those opponents who've been crushing you, but you can start beating those players who used to beat you 6-4, 6-3.

You will have to make changes. In many instances you will have to think and act somewhat differently on the court. Getting better is easy, but it is not effortless. You will have to be willing to make mistakes and occasionally take a short step back in order to take two long steps forward.

You will make errors. You may even lose a few sets that you might have won "your old way." That's okay. The one thing for sure is that if you don't try to change and improve your tennis, you will never get better.

# SET SMART GOALS

If you are reading this book your tennis goal is probably to win more often and have more fun on the court. To achieve this overall goal, you can create literally an unlimited number of smaller goals — different goals for each day or week or season.

By setting these smaller, realistic, individual goals, you can experience numerous successes on the court — successes which may or may not have to do with winning one particular match on any given day.

For example, you may decide that in the next set of tennis you play, your goal is to move your feet more. No matter what else happens in that set, if you actually moved your feet more than you usually do, then you "win" in the sense that you accomplished your goal. You established a small goal, you met that goal, and now you can build from there.

Another day you might say, "Okay I'm going to still try to move my feet more, but I'm going to concentrate on playing one step closer to the net than I usually do to receive serve."

Again, if you remember to move a step closer for each return, even if this throws your return off at first, then you "win" again. You will have accomplished another one of your goals.

The wonderful aspect of accomplishing a number of easy, small goals is that this will result in the accomplishment of your ultimate tennis goal: You will win more often and have more fun on the court.

# SEEK SENSIBLE SOLUTIONS

Attaining your goals and becoming a more effective tennis player is easier than many people believe. This does not mean, however, that the road to improvement is problem-free. What it means is that you have to deal with the problems you have and the problems you meet along the way in an intelligent manner.

The solutions to these problems must be realistic and sensible. The "problems" simply offer you opportunities to become a better, more sensible tennis player.

In a very real sense, becoming a more effective tennis player is a matter of brains over brawn. It is easier to play "smarter" tennis than "better" tennis." It is easier to hit "smarter" shots than "better" shots.

A big serve or blasting forehand or delicate drop shot will not be the biggest weapons in your tennis arsenal; your brain is and will always be your most potent weapon.

This book has many, many, many hints, tips, strategies, and suggestions to improve your tennis game. Be selective. Obviously not every reader can or should incorporate every suggestion into his or her game. Try to pick and choose and experiment and remember not every "hint" is for every player.

The next page contains a "case study." Case studies will be used throughout the book. Names have been changed to protect the guilty, and any resemblance to you, your tennis game, or players you know is purely coincidental.

In all the case studies the player or perhaps the team has a "situation," a problem that might be solved a number of different ways. The solutions offered by this book are often simple, straightforward, and easy to accomplish.

# A CASE STUDY

Fireball Flannagan is a 4.0 player who recently had his first serve clocked at 107 mph at the local shopping mall. One of Fireball's problems with winning in the real world is that his first serve, although great, goes into the court only about one out of five times.

His second serve is a floater that is successfully attacked by his opponents. He's actually **losing** close matches because of his great serve.

**An Impractical Solution:** Set aside a few hours a day to work on getting a 107 mph serve in more often, while simultaneously developing, practicing, and getting total confidence in a high–kicking second serve that can be placed deep to the opponent's backhand. Achieving this solution, however, might take ten months to ten years and the realistic chances of effective completion for Flannagan are somewhere below slim.

**A Practical Solution:** Take about 30 percent of the speed off the first serve and work on having the motion and rhythm of the first and second serves become similar. Don't try for a rocket on the first serve, but try similar serves, one just a little stronger than the other. Change the emphasis from speed to depth, location, and consistency. This practical solution could be accomplished in a couple of days to a couple of weeks. Flannagan has all the physical skills; he really only needs a little discipline and a little practice.

# COACH, I'VE ALREADY GOT A FEW QUESTIONS

**"I'm already a little nervous. There looks like a lot of stuff to read here. Do I need to be real smart to use this book?"**

No. It is easy, friendly stuff. Plus, you can read it in ten days or ten weeks or ten years. The idea is to have fun with the book as you are getting better.

**"Coach, I play a lot with a person who continually gives everyone horrible calls. It makes the game 'no fun.' What do you suggest?"**

Easy. Dump the dork. If this person is really making the game "no fun," don't play with this dork.

**"Coach, I notice later in the book you talk about the drop shot. I can't hit that shot at all."**

That's okay. It's a tough shot, but you can practice hitting a drop shot by yourself. Just stand near the service line and bounce the ball and hit it over the net. And you can also forget about the drop shot. There's other stuff you can work on.

**"Coach, aren't you limiting my potential if you say I'll never hit shots like the pros?"**

You may be able to hit shots like the pros, but you probably won't hit shots like the pros consistently. That is a fact. Your potential for improvement, however, remains basically limitless.

# "NEVER KICK A FRESH TURD ON A HOT DAY"

*Those words of wisdom came from President Harry S. Truman. Hopefully they do not have a lot of applications on the tennis courts where you play. But perhaps the following list of "nevers" can help you.*

**NEVER** . . . hit any shot as hard as you can. Tennis is not a power game, and if you are trying to hit a shot as hard as you can, the natural flow of the stroke is destroyed. Most of the time you'll make an error.

**NEVER** . . . think or say to yourself "I'VE GOT TO GET THIS SHOT IN!" (serve, return, volley, overhead, any shot). Who needs this kind of pressure? Rather KNOW you'll get the shot in and concentrate on a smooth, relaxed execution. Practice this attitude. It works.

**NEVER** . . . let your heels touch the court. From before the ball is served until the point is over, you should be moving, bouncing, dancing on the balls of your feet. If you do this, you'll not only cover the court better, but the quality of your shots will also be better.

**NEVER** . . . bend from the waist for the low ball. Instead, bend from the knees. Bending the knees is magic. It gives your shots power and stability, takes stress off your arm and back, and sends shots over and in that otherwise wouldn't make it.

**NEVER** . . . become more interested in "beating" the opponent than in winning the match. Keep your ultimate goal clear. Don't let personalities cloud your mind.

**NEVER** ... backpedal for an overhead! You want to get your racquet and yourself back early for an overhead, but don't back up. Instead drop your foot back and slide sideways. It is faster, easier, and safer.

**NEVER** ... go after a shot if your partner has called for it, even if it is the stupidest call in the history of tennis. It is better to lose the point than to have both players trying to return the same shot. (It also reduces the number of visits to the emergency room.)

**NEVER** ... do anything on the tennis court that you wouldn't be happy to tell your mother about the next day. Or your father or your wife or husband or kids.

---

### WINSTON CHURCHILL'S "NEVER"

Here's one "never" you might try to practice each time you step onto the court: It was suggested over a half century ago, and Winston Churchill was talking of something much more important than tennis. Still, the determination and the message might help you on the court as well as off.

**"Never give in,
never, never, never, never."**

*Three more "nevers" that might help you inside or outside the fence:*

"Never pick a fight with an inanimate object."
– *P. J. O'Rourke*
"Never take the antidote before the poison."
– *Unknown*
"Never be haughty to the humble. Never be
humble to the haughty."
– *Jefferson Davis*

# SOME REALLY STUPID THINGS PEOPLE SAY

*You've never said these things yourself, of course . . . but you may have heard other players utter these gems.*

**"My first serve is great. It doesn't go in very often, but it is great."**
Hello? If the first serve doesn't go in very often, it is not great. There may be an occasional great first serve, but that is quite different.

**"It was a perfect drop shot, but it just caught the top of the net and didn't quite make it over."**
Hello again? Perfect shots win rather than lose the point. What is being described is an unforced error, not a perfect drop shot.

**"They just hit winning shots for the entire match."**
Doubtful, at best. Probably "they" were much more effective players, but just as probably the losing team's errors outnumbered the winning team's winners.

**"It wasn't my fault. My partner just didn't hold serve once during the whole match."**
The TEAM holds serve, not just the server. As often as not it is the server's partner's fault that the server couldn't hold serve. Whatever the reality is in this situation, don't ever blame a partner for a loss.

# CHAPTER 3

# SHARPENING YOUR STROKES

*"It's not how you hold your racquet, it's how you hold your mind."*
*– Perry Jones*

The "strokes" in tennis are simply the mechanics of hitting the tennis ball — the way you use your racquet and your body to make the ball move over the net.

The philosophy is that the more consistent and mechanically correct your strokes are, the better your shots will be. That is a tough philosophy to argue with . . .

. . . but the truth is that most people do not develop fluid, picturesque, beautiful-to-watch strokes. You hit the ball the way you hit the ball.

You may know what you "should" do, but you have your own unique strokes. And the longer you have been playing, the harder it becomes to change these strokes.

So as Perry Jones's quote suggests, your state of mind is probably more important than the state of your strokes. That is what much of this book is trying to reinforce.

This does not mean you shouldn't bother trying to improve your strokes. It just means your goals in this area should be realistic and attainable. Unquestionably, the best way to work on stroke production over the long term is with your local teaching pro.

Below are some general concepts and basic reminders about the strokes. Following each general description of the mechanics of a certain stroke are a few troubleshooting ideas that can help you help yourself between sessions with your teaching pro.

## THE SERVE

The service motion is perhaps the most personal and unique signature stroke for any player. You've all seen the windmill serve, the pirouette, the shot put, and even the vegematic server who seems to slice, dice, and julienne the serve.

Whatever your own serve actually looks like, however you actually stroke the serve, several basics apply.

First, the serve is the only time you are allowed to try to toss the ball where you want it to be. So practice your toss. Concentrate on getting your toss where you want it with a slow, even motion.

Next, remember to use your shoulders and legs for consistency on the serve. You should not think of serving with your arm. You should think of stroking the serve with your whole body.

Also, try to keep the stroke of your first and second serves close to the same motion and rhythm. Most humans don't have enough time to practice one service motion, let alone two very different ones.

Here are some ideas to think about if your serve is not working as well as you would like it to.

**\* If you're having problems with consistency** — Slow everything down to two-thirds speed. Make sure your legs and shoulders are involved in this slow-motion service stroke.

**\* If you're tight, not fluid** — Shake yourself. Loosen your wrist and your arm, your whole body. Take a deep breath and let it out. Bend your knees a couple of times. Tell yourself a joke. Although other strokes will require a firm wrist, the serve does not. Relax your wrist and relax your whole body and just let the serve happen.

**\* If your timing seems off** — Eliminate the take-back by already starting back. Try starting with the racquet in the "backscratching position." It is just a way of simplifying the service motion and timing. Some very good players serve like this all the time. Remember to use your legs and shoulders.

**\* If you're faulting into the net** — Think of hitting the serve up, not down. Make sure your serve is clearing the net by at least two feet. And vow never to fault into the net again. No kidding here. You can hit the ball into the fence, but never into the net.

**\* If you have been "over-thinking" the serve** — Practice the "I don't give a _ _ _ t" drill from time to time. In practice, simply hit a bunch of loose, sloppy serves while saying "I don't give a hoot." It can loosen up the stroke and help your rhythm — and the large number of well-hit serves will scare you. Sometime when you are loose and don't give a hoot where the serve is going, it goes exactly where it is supposed to!

# THE GROUND STROKES, FOREHAND AND BACKHAND

The very first time you picked up a tennis racquet and walked on the court you were probably advised to "keep your eye on the ball" and "take your racquet back early." This instructional advice you first heard about the ground strokes is probably still the most important. No matter how good your stroke is, you have to be watching the moving object you are going to use it on (the ball) and you have to be ready to use the stroke.

So, why doesn't everyone do these two basic things?

**First, most players do not understand what "keeping your eye on the ball" really means.** It is much more than just watching or looking at the ball. It is an intense visual concentration on the ball from the time it leaves your opponent's racquet until you see it hit the strings of your racquet.

**Second, two-thirds of the time you can get away with a late backswing, so you get lazy.** You get away with late preparation on two shots and then get surprised by a third deeper or stronger shot, and you make an error.

Interestingly, to incorporate these two exceptionally important basics into your game is more like establishing a good habit than developing a skill. Not everyone can hit a strong backhand, spin serve, or wonderful drop shot, but anyone and everyone can improve visual concentration and racquet preparation.

**If you did nothing else but improve your visual concentration on the ball and get your racquet back earlier, you would have better ground strokes.**

# THE FOREHAND

The forehand stroke should be natural and use your body's natural rotation and weight-shift. As with all the strokes, you stroke the ball with your whole body, not just your arm. You want to move your racquet through the ball at a medium speed and be sure to follow through smoothly.

Remember that in order to use your forehand stroke consistently, your feet have to get you into position to stroke the shot. Don't reach for shots with your arm; get there with your feet

Despite the fact that most club players favor their forehand, it is a stroke that can suddenly begin causing you problems. Here are some things to try if your forehand goes awry.

* **If the ball is flying all over the place** — Try to slow down the racquet speed and lengthen the follow-through. Try to keep the racquet strings and the ball together longer.

* **If there seems to be "nothing behind" your forehand** — Try placing the fingers of your left hand on the inside of your right elbow, loosely. Hit some easy forehands at medium speed. Yes, you'll feel weird, but this will get more shoulder rotation and less arm into the forehand. It can help you to stop swinging across your chest, which weakens the stroke.

* **If you suspect your wrist may be causing mechanical breakdowns** — Try putting a wristband on your wrist (two if you already wear one) to remind you to keep your wrist firm throughout the shot. Sounds simple, but it can help.

* **If the ball seems never to be in the right place** — Concentrate on moving your feet more. Take small, quick steps. These steps help your body to get in the best position to hit your stroke. Even perfect

strokes won't work if your legs don't put your body, the racquet, and the ball in the right place to use the stroke.

# THE BACKHAND

The backhand is not the favorite stroke of most club players. In fact, many players seem to have made it a life's mission to avoid backhands. Through creative positioning and by running around their backhands, they manage to have to hit a backhand only once a month or so.

The mechanics of the backhand are actually simpler than the forehand. Your body is not in the way. The reason it is not the favorite is because it is hit much less often, and most players lack confidence in the stroke.

There is no mystery to this stroke. Early preparation, concentration, and a smooth weight transfer are the keys, just as with the forehand. A reliable, boring slice backhand or a safe medium-speed two-hander is all that most players will ever need. The backhand is rarely the reason a match is won or lost.

No matter how you hit the backhand or with how many hands, if you're having some trouble, here are some helpful thoughts or reminders for this side.

* **If you are feeling rushed** — Use both hands to take your racquet back on the backhand side. Whether you hit with one or two, taking the racquet back with two will help you get prepared with your shoulders turned and racquet back sooner.

* **If you are playing against a weak server** — Position yourself to take the serve as a backhand. When you are expecting a backhand (not hoping one won't come), your stroke will be more fluid and relaxed. You'll get practice and build confidence.

**\* If you feel yourself reaching or stretching to hit** — As with the forehand, make sure your footwork is putting you in the best position to use your stroke. Quicker, smaller steps can often be all that an ailing backhand needs to cure it.

**\* If your backhands seem to "pop" off your racquet** — Work on developing a longer follow-through by thinking about sailing a paper plate or Frisbee. The motion is probably natural for you, but sometimes putting a racquet in your hand can tighten you up.

## THE VOLLEY

The volley should be easy. If the body would do what the mind told it to do, everyone would be a great volleyer. The mechanics of this stroke are simple: You just step in and block the ball back over the net. It is more a matter of timing than mechanics.

The problem is that most players move the racquet much more than they need to and move their feet much less than they need to when they are volleying.

Here are a few suggestions for the volley, if you're having trouble with this "simple stroke."

**\* If you are swinging too much** — Put your racquet down. Have someone hit or throw you the ball and step across and catch it. Repeat catching it a dozen or so times. Pick up the racquet and try to step across and catch it with the racquet.

**\* If you are still taking that racquet back too far** — Put on the handcuffs. Place one wristband around both wrists and practice hitting volleys. This should stop you from swinging and help you to meet the volley in front.

**\* If your volleys lack authority** — Here's another trick to get you to contact the volley in front and early. Stand a racquet's length from the net and have someone feed you shots. Step in and make contact on your opponent's side of the net — before the ball even gets to your side. You'll hit great volleys. Now, just step back and volley the same way without reaching over the net.

**\* If you are popping up those low volleys** — Bend from your knees, not your waist, to get down low with the shots.

**\* If you are miss-hitting too many volleys** — Try the "handcuffs" again and make sure you are making contact in front where you can see the ball. Miss-hits are often the result of letting the ball get too far back where you can't see it.

## THE OVERHEAD

The overhead is mechanically similar to the serve. The problem is you don't get to place the ball where you want. In fact, as has been mentioned, your opponent is intent on placing the ball exactly where you do not want it.

Positioning and a little practice are the keys to getting a good, consistent stroke on the overhead. If you are in position behind the ball and ready to hit, and if you've practiced enough to be confident with your swing, then it will work.

But just in case you run into some trouble, here are several suggestions that you can try.

**\* If you seem to be hitting the ball well but it is not going in the court** — Make sure your shoulders are turned perpendicular to the net as soon as you know the ball is being lobbed. If your shoulders are parallel to the net, you will make more errors. Period.

**\* If you are hitting the ball "a ton" but it doesn't seem to**

**be going over and in** — Then try hitting it at "half a ton" with a smoother stroke. Remember, the goal is a quality shot, not the hardest shot ever hit by a human.

* **If you tend to take your eye off the ball** — Use your non- racquet hand to point at the ball and keep watching the ball as you hit it. Keep your eye on the ball until you actually hit it. There is no hurry to see where it is going.

* **If the lobs are getting over your head so you can't get a good swing** — Practice anticipating when the ball is about to be lobbed and "cheat" by getting into position sooner. Being in position with your racquet back is really the key to a consistent overhead, even if the actual mechanics of the stroke are less than pretty.

# THE LOB

The lob is mechanically a cousin of the ground strokes (forehand or backhand). The goal of the shot is different, however, which makes the mechanics slightly different. The lob is not a "pop" or "jab," it is a stroke that is supposed to get the ball higher in the air.

If you are having trouble with the lob, here are some things you might try the next time you're on the court.

* **If you don't have a clue where your lob is going** — Try shortening your backswing slightly. Lift the ball from this shorter backswing but remember to keep your follow-through long and smooth and to use your whole body.

* **If your lob is going long too often** — You are probably trying to lob "too deep." The stroke is fine, but you are trying to lob the ball over your opponents' head instead of making them hit an overhead.

* **If you don't seem to have any "feel" for your lob** — Remember

you need your legs and body in the stroke. You don't need them for power but rather for control, consistency, and confidence.

# THE DROP SHOT

The drop shot is like a mini-lob. It's a lift up and over the net. And, as with the lob, a short backswing and complete follow-through are the keys to success with the drop shot.

It is a special shot that can become an important weapon in your arsenal. And remember the drop shot does not have to be a winner to be effective.

If you don't own an effective, proven drop shot, you probably shouldn't even try one in a match. To help you develop or tune up your drop shot, the following might help.

* **Practice the drop shot's mechanics by yourself.** Simply bounce the ball and try to experiment with the stroke — a little more sidespin, a little more underspin. Just play with it for a couple of minutes by softly making contact with the ball. You don't even need a net or tennis court.

* **Try your backhand drop shot.** It may not be your favorite ground stroke, but you may find it will work in executing the drop, so experiment from both sides.

* **Use your body.** Remember, even though it is a soft stroke you must use your feet to get into position and your legs and body to execute it correctly.

* **Practice the mechanics of the drop shot.** Stand at mid-court just bouncing a ball and hit a drop shot over the net and into a wastebasket that you have placed seven or eight feet away from the net on the other side of the court.

# TWO CASE STUDIES

## A CASE STUDY

**The Situation:** Kelly has a great cross-court forehand. It is a solid consistent shot. The problem is everyone on the court knows it will be going cross-court. When Kelly tries to alter the stroke to hit down the line the result is too many errors.

**The Problem:** Kelly doesn't have to alter the good forehand stroke to hit it down the line. In fact, trying to alter the stroke is what is causing the errors.

**The Solution:** To hit the forehand down the line all Kelly has to do is turn a little bit more sideways. By simply remembering to turn the hips and shoulders more, Kelly was able to use the existing forehand stroke to add a new dimension to the game.

## ANOTHER CASE STUDY

**The Situation:** Dale is a good athlete, moves well, and has excellent technique. The problem is that when closing in on the net all the opponent's shots seem to handcuff Dale. The volleys become ineffective.

**The Problem:** Dale knows where the opponent's shots are going and is simply running in to them as if to catch them with the hands instead of the racquet.

**The Solution:** Having figured out the problem, the solution was easy. Dale had to slow down the approach to the net a little so as not to overrun the shot, to hesitate and concentrate on the timing and approach. The volleying technique was just fine, the positioning just needed some adjustment.

# COACH, SOME OF THIS STUFF'S NOT WORKING!

**"Coach, I am moving more and bouncing on the balls of my feet and it works. But I only last about one set before I'm exhausted."**

Good. If you have your doctor's okay, hang in there. If you are constantly moving and not starting and stopping all the time you should actually conserve energy after a while.

**"Coach, this one team always kills us with great lobs that go over our heads every time."**

Well, if this is actually true and these opponents are beating you with lobs, then make them "kill" you with something else. Play farther from the net. Anticipate the lob. Start back earlier. Do not let them beat you by lobbing.

**"Coach, I'm moving into the volley more, but it's causing my volleys to go long."**

Maybe, but check to make sure you aren't also swinging at these volleys. Also check to be sure your racquet head is angled so your volley is getting some underspin for control.

**"Coach, my opponents are hitting some shots you said they couldn't."**

Probably not many. But the deal wasn't that they couldn't hit low-percentage shots ever. The deal was they would not be able to hit these low-percentage shots consistently.

# TRUE OR FALSE?

*Following are ten true-false questions. You can check your answers on the next page. You can cheat if you want to. If you don't like tests, just skip it.*

**1. True or False?** After consistency the next most important thing to strive for with the serve is speed.

**2. True or False?** The most effective place to be to receive serve is about a foot or two behind the baseline.

**3. True or False?** The primary and most important job of the server's partner is to protect the alley.

**4. True or False?** The objective of a "drop shot" is to hit the ball just barely over the net, so your opponent can't get to it.

**5. True or False?** The least effective part of most players' games is the backhand ground stroke.

**6. True or False?** When rushing the net, a player should run to a step or two inside the service line and take a "split-step" or hesitate before hitting the first volley or half-volley.

**7. True or False?** The rule of thumb is that the strongest, most consistent returner of serve should play the ad court.

**8. True or False?** A good rule in doubles when you are at the net is to let a ball driven by your opponent go if it is going to your partner's forehand.

**9. True or False?** Anyone on the court can call a "let." It is an excellent call after a short lob by your partner.

**10. True or False?** When you're in trouble in a point, the drop shot is often a great shot to get you out of trouble.

# ANSWERS

**1. FALSE.** Depth and/or placement of your serve are the next goal after consistency.

**2. FALSE.** That's probably too far back. Right about the baseline is a good place to start, but you want to be as far inside the baseline as you can be on any given serve.

**3. FALSE.** The primary goal of the server's partner is to "get into the head" of the receiver.

**4. FALSE.** The objective of the drop shot is to move the opponent into the net to hit a difficult shot. If you are trying to make it a winner, you'll make too many errors.

**5. FALSE, PROBABLY.** The backhand overhead or even just the overhead are less effective shots for many players.

**6. FALSE.** You approach the net until a certain time (not to a certain place). The time your opponent makes contact with the ball is when you take your split-step or hesitate to see where the heck it is going.

**7. TRUE.** There can be other considerations, but the most important shot for the receiving team is the return of serve, and the most important returns will be hit from the ad court.

**8. FALSE.** A good rule in doubles when you're at the net is to have the person closer to the net play the drive.

**9. TRUE AND FALSE.** Anyone on the court can call a "let" for any legitimate reason. Your partner's weak lob doesn't, unfortunately, constitute a legitimate reason.

**10. FALSE.** Don't ever try a drop shot when you are in trouble. Instead, throw up . . . a defensive lob.

# CHAPTER 4

# HITTING SMARTER SHOTS

*"I think if people could hear what the coaches are saying, they would realize there is a lot more to this game than just hitting the ball."*
*– Andre Agassi*

Didn't we just do the shots? Nope. We just did the strokes.

The strokes have to do with the mechanics of hitting the ball. The shots have to do with what happens after you stroke it — where the ball is going and how it is going there. The stroke takes place on your side of the net. The shot is what the ball does on the other side of the net after you have stroked it.

And as Mr. Agassi points out above, tennis is much more than hitting shots. It is about hitting smarter shots!

Your strokes may be ugly enough to make teaching pros cry and small children run from the courts. But if somehow you hit the shots over and to the right places to force errors and win points, then you are hitting good shots. So forget about the mechanics of the strokes for a while and look at what you want to have happen to the shots.

# THE SERVE

The serve is the shot that begins the point. It is not supposed to end the point. And as there are no points awarded in tennis for style, there are also no points awarded for speed.

An effective server, like a good baseball pitcher or a good debater, keeps the opponent off balance. Your serve should keep the receiver guessing, out of sync, and unable to establish a rhythm on the return. This is achieved not by serving fast but by serving smart.

Here are some ideas to make your serve, no matter how you stroke it, a better, smarter shot.

* **Serve deep in the service box.** The farther away from the net you can keep a receiver the less effective the return and the more time you have to get ready for it.

* **Move your serve around.** Right, left, down the middle. Make your opponents move. Make them stand still. Keep them guessing. Never serve to the same spot twice in a row.

* **Assume your serve is going in.** Plan on it going in. Don't even think about it going out or into the net. If you expect it to go in, it will go in — more often. This is not New Age mumbo jumbo. It is fact.

* **Try to think your serve to a certain area of the service box** every single time you serve. You don't aim it to an area of the court, you just "think" it there. It will not go where you want it to

every time, and that's okay. Again, no mumbo jumbo. This works with a little practice.

\* **Don't admire your serve** or strain to see whether it's in or out. Instead, serve and then go visually to the receiver's racquet. If the ball is coming back, that's where it will come from, and if you're paying attention you'll know how and where. You'll be ready sooner.

\* **Bounce on the balls of your feet** after you serve. If you are on your toes, you will almost automatically get into position to hit your next shot.

\* **Use the old one-two combination.** Use your serve and your "return of the return" as a combination. Have a plan each time you serve. A plan not only for the serve but for your next shot as well. Yes, you can do this.

\* **Practice your serve by yourself.** You don't need a court or a net or a partner. And remember, practice translates to confidence, and confidence is what the serve is all about.

## THE RETURN OF SERVE

Just as with the serve, the purpose of the return of serve is NOT to win the point. The purpose is to get the ball back in play. You want your return to be as offensive, pressing, and difficult for your opponent as is possible off any given serve. At the same time you would like to put one hundred percent of your returns into play.

A fairly realistic goal for your return of serve is to have the server know that you will put the ball back in play every single time, that there will be no cheap points for the server!

The following reminders will help make your return of serve a more effective shot and maybe help you break serve more often.

**\* Be consistent.** You want to get your return over and in every time. You do not want two brilliant winners and then two errors. Consistency is the key. Give the server endless opportunities to make errors. Keep up the pressure.

**\* Return serve within your capabilities.** You can't expect to execute better shots than those you own.

**\* Make the server serve the ball where you want to receive it.** It is amazingly simple. Use your positioning and your body language to control where the server will try to hit the ball. If you set up way right, chances are the server will aim way left. Try it.

**\* Have a specific return in mind.** Since you can cause the serve to be hit to a certain place, have a return in mind before the server even serves it. Sure, the actual serve may change your plans. That's okay.

**\* Play in as close as you can** to comfortably return the serve, and start your feet moving before the serve is hit. Move into the shot. By doing this you'll be able to return the ball to the server earlier and shorten the server's preparation time and rush the server on the "return of the return."

**\* Get your shoulder turned** and take your racquet back as soon as you know whether the serve will be to your right or your left. You can't take your racquet back too early, and most of us take it back too late way too often.

**\* Block back very strong serves.** Don't try to meet power with power. You don't have time for a long stroke. Just use the server's power to block it back (almost like a volley).

**\* Use your return to control** the point, game, set, and match. Don't worry about winners. Do your best to develop a "one hundred percenter," a never-fail return.

# THE VOLLEY

The volley is a wonderful example of a shot that can be, and often is, hit very effectively with a very odd or unique stroke.

Since the volleyer is close to the net and is in effect taking the speed from the opponent's shot and simply blocking it back into the opponent's court, the job is fairly easy.

An effective volleyer does not have to be fast, or have quick hands, or have great technique. An effective volleyer does have to have a slight understanding of basic geometry and be willing to give away a point or two to win ten.

The volley is a shot where most club players can make huge improvements in effectiveness. And happily, you can make these improvements with the skills and physical techniques you already have in your repertoire.

So if you want to have some fun and wake up your net game a little, try some of these ideas.

* **Move your feet more** and your arm and racquet less. If this is all you do, you will probably be a better volleyer.

* **Cut down your opponents' passing angle** by moving in front of your opponents when they are hitting the ball. Then readjust your position after your next shot.

* **Angle volleys sharp and short** if there is an open court.

* **Volley straight ahead deep** if an obvious angled opening does not exist or if you are back from the net.

* **Volley down the middle deep anytime.**

* **"Cheat" at the net.** Much of the time when you are at the net you will sense where the ball will be coming, whether it will be a forehand or backhand volley. Cheat to that side. Anticipate and be ready sooner and you will execute better. Yes, you'll get fooled once in a while. It's okay.

* **Look through the strings of your racquet** at the ball when you volley. This should not only remind you to concentrate visually on the ball but also to make contact with the ball early and out in front.

# THE FIRST (TRANSITIONAL) VOLLEY

The first or transitional volley is the volley you have to execute when you are moving from the back court to the net. The differences between this volley and a regular volley are basically that you are on the move more and you will probably be farther away from the net than you would like to be.

Perhaps the key to executing this shot is to be in control of your body and not be moving too fast into the net. A hesitation or split-step will help you get into control as your opponent hits the ball. You are far better off being in control and in less than the perfect position than being in a great position but moving like a lunatic.

Use a few of the following ideas to execute a better first volley.

* **Watch the ball** as it comes off your opponent's racquet. Even though you are on the move, don't forget this basic. It enables you to read where the ball is going.

* **Move into the shot** after your split-step or hesitation. Don't stop and wait for it. You must move into the shot to control it.

* **Get down low with your knees** and stay down with the shot. Don't pop up like a jack-in-the-box.

**\* Don't be afraid of this volley.** It is a difficult shot but that's what makes it fun.

**\* Forget sharp angles on this volley.** You are probably too far from the net. Play it safe.

**\* Play this volley safe and smart.** Don't even think about a winner. Play it deep and prepare for your next shot. You do not want highlight film shots with your first volley.

**\* Close in on the net after this volley.** Remember it is a transitional volley on your way to a good position at the net.

# THE OVERHEAD

People often refer to this shot as the "overhead smash," which is probably why there are so many unforced errors on this shot. The word "smash" seems to make too many people try to hit too many overheads too hard.

Yes, if you're in position, you want an offensive shot but you shouldn't try to over-hit this shot. A quality, medium-speed overhead hit to the percentage area of the court should be your goal.

Forget about smashing the shot and use your feet and your head to execute better overheads.

Try these suggestions to get the most out of your overhead.

**\* Get into position.** Remember, hitting an effective overhead has a great deal to do with being in good position — behind the ball with your racquet back.

**\* Use a sharp angle wisely.** Angle your overhead only if you are well inside the service line and the angle really exists.

**\* Go deep with your overhead.** If there is no easy, fat angle available, or if you are hitting from the service line or deeper, hit your overhead as deep as possible.

**\* Don't try to avoid hitting an overhead** toward an opponent at net. Don't try to hit anyone, but if the percentage overhead is cross-court, don't try to hit a more difficult shot to be polite.

**\* Try moving back a few steps.** Line up farther from the net if you're struggling with overheads. This should get you in better position to hit your overhead.

**\* Play a safe overhead anytime you're not ready** or out of sync or in any trouble. Slow and deep will give you a chance to get back in the point.

# THE LOB

There are two basic types of lobs — defensive and offensive. Use a defensive lob when you or your team are in trouble. Use it when you're on the run and that's about all you can do, and when you need some time to regroup or get back in position. The idea is to hit it high and hope.

Offensive lobs, at the club level, are all the other lobs you hit. Offensive does not mean you are trying to win the point with that lob. It is an offensive lob because you are using it as part of your offensive game plan to control the match.

Mixing a few offensive lobs into your game can make all your shots more effective. The following are some suggestions for better lobs.

**\* Stay in control.** Leave those magnificent topspin lobs to the pros.

**\* Remember, you do not have to try to get your lob over the net**

**person's head** and have it bounce. You just have to force the net person to move back and hit a difficult shot.

* **Make your opponent work.** Lob a few times in a row against an opponent at net who is volleying well, poaching, hitting winning volleys. A few lobs will make this opponent work a little harder and keep them honest up there.

* **Lob when it is not expected.** Surprise your opponents with a quick lob when they thought you were about to kill it.

* **Use the lob in combination** with a short, low ball to make your opponents work a bit.

* **Remember you are not trying to win the point with the lob.** If you do, that's great. Just don't try to.

# THE DROP SHOT

The drop shot is a weapon that you should use sparingly. The object of the drop shot is not to hit a ball your opponent can't get to (although if that happens you won't be unhappy). The object of the drop shot is to make your opponent have to cover a lot of the court to get to the shot and then to have to play it defensively after getting there and use a lot of energy.

Here are some reminders for better drop shots.

* **Clear the net with your drop shot.** Even if it bounces on the service line, you're still in the point. If it goes into the net, you are not. You just lost the point.

* **Attempt a drop shot only if you're well inside the baseline.** There is no percentage in even trying a drop shot from behind the baseline — too difficult and too much time for your opponent.

**\* Hit a drop shot only when you are in control,** and your opponent is not expecting it. Do not try the drop shot to get you out of trouble.

**\* Remember, if your drop shot goes to the middle of the court,** it will come back over the middle. If you go to one side or the other, your opponent may need more steps to get to the shot but may have two choices on the return.

**\* Use the drop shot and lob combination as suggested above.** Even if you lose the point, you are making your opponent expend a whole lot of energy.

---

# A CASE STUDY

**The Situation:** Betty B. is right-handed and has a great forehand volley and loves to poach and play aggressively when her partner is serving to the deuce court.

**The Problem:** Unfortunately Betty B. has no confidence in her backhand volley so when the serve is to the ad court she stands in the alley like a statue. Since the important points are played on this side, she is costing her team some close matches.

**The Solution:** Betty should move anyway. She should pretend she is going to poach or poach even if she loses a point. She needs to be a factor in both receivers' minds.

She could also try playing in the Australian Formation on a few of these ad court serves. This means Betty B. can use her forehand volley and possibly also confuse the opponents a little bit.

---

# A FATHER'S LESSON IN LEARNING

*This man and his young daughter seemed always to have time for practicing tennis together. She was a sponge. She asked questions and listened and practiced and learned quickly from her dad.*

*But children have a way of growing up, and soon the daughter was a thousand miles away at school.*

*One Christmas vacation this man and his daughter were on the tennis court — hitting together, practicing, so that the daughter, now 16, might make her school team.*

*They hit for a while and then decided to play a set. The father hoped he might share some of his experience, his tennis insights, so that he might help her play smarter tennis.*

*They played. The father chipped a few returns and followed them to net. The daughter hit some good drives, but the old man volleyed them away.*

*"Why don't you try a lob once in a while so I can't close in on the net so tightly," he suggested.*

*"My lob sucks," she proclaimed. "I can't lob."*

*They took a time-out. He discussed the idea and execution of the lob, the technique, and the timing. They even hit a dozen or so practice lobs. They resumed play, and as he approached the net after their time-out the teenage daughter proved beyond any doubt that her lob "sucked."*

*She lobbed long, wide, into the next court. Into the next county. "I told you I couldn't lob!" she said. Case closed.*

*They practiced and played a few more times that vacation. They worked on many things, especially the lob. There was some progress, but the "old dad" often felt he might be talking only to himself.*

*The vacation ended. The father and the daughter said good-bye once again. She was soon back at school and she did make the team. That summer, home for a week before her job started, the young woman asked her father if he wanted to hit some tennis balls. He was delighted.*

*They hit for a while and started a set. On one of his daughter's short second serves the father closed in on the net. Her lob carried over his left shoulder, out of reach and well inside the baseline.*

*His next service game he followed a big serve into the net. She chipped a low, slow return right at his feet. He made the difficult volley, but her next lob was up and over him before he could recover, and he butchered the overhead.*

*The set continued pretty much this way: a lobbing clinic for the father. When the "clinic" ended, he was both thoroughly exhausted and proud. His daughter had played well and lobbed almost perfectly.*

*"That was great," the father wheezed. "Those lobs were magnificent! Where did you learn to lob like that?" he asked with a knowing smile.*

*She looked at him quizzically and replied, "Lobs? I don't know, I guess I must have learned at school."*

# TENNIS FACT OR TENNIS FICTION?

**1. When your opponent is rushing the net, your objective should be a crisp, passing shot.**
FICTION: The percentage shot here is simply to make your opponent have to execute this transitional volley. Try to keep the ball low to force the volley up.

**2. The best way to control or negate a good poacher at the net is to hit a passing shot down the alley.**
FICTION: That is exactly one of the things the poacher is trying to get you to do. It is a low percentage shot. Probably the best way to neutralize an effective poacher is to put up some low lobs over the non-racquet shoulder. This backs the poacher away from the net a bit and forces some awkward overheads.

**3. The return of serve is the most important shot in tennis.**
FACT: Well, probably a fact. The conventional wisdom says the serve is the most important shot, but at the club level a very convincing argument can be made for the return of serve as the most important. Okay, they're both "most important."

**4. Pete Sampras is the greatest men's player of all time.**
Just having you on a bit. There is no definitive way to decide the greatest of all time. And Americans seem overly concerned with "Number One" anyway. So let's just say Sampras is one of the greatest along with Laver, Borg, Agassi, Federer, and many many others.

# COACH, I NEED SOME HELP HERE!

**"Coach, my partner is giving bad calls to our opponents. Shots that hit even in front of the line he sometimes calls "out." What do I do?"**

You have to talk to him about his calls and explain that unless both teammates see a shot as "out" then that shot is "in." If it is his eyesight, maybe you should call the shots. If it is not his eyesight.....

**"Coach when I take a lesson with my teaching pro I can get into a groove and start hitting great ground strokes. Somehow, in a match these strokes seem to disappear."**

Your consistent strokes haven't disappeared. You are playing in a match where your opponents are trying to keep you off balance so you can't find your groove. In the teaching situation the pro was feeding you balls so you could find your groove. Next session with the pro ask if you could work on the strokes under more matchlike conditions.

**"An old friend and I decided after years of being couch potatoes, we would start playing tennis again. We're too out of shape to play singles, but we don't want to play doubles quite yet."**

Glad you decided to get back on the court. You don't have to play "regular" singles. The two of you can start out with mini tennis or ghost doubles or make up your own games and rules on the court.

# CHAPTER 5

# HITTING SPECIAL SHOTS

*"I played some pretty special shots today. I thought I did eveything really well."*
*– Andy Murray*

If the previous two chapters could be considered as dealing with the "meat and potatoes" of tennis, then this chapter is perhaps the appetizer, or dessert, or an after-dinner drink.

Many very good players go a lifetime without mastering some of the specialty shots mentioned in this chapter. But if you are fortunate enough to occasionally have a match where you "play some pretty special shots" like Andy Murray did against Andy Roddick at Wimbledon in 2006, well, then maybe these shots are worth a bit of practice.

Maybe you'll even perfect some of these shots and add a secret weapon or two to your arsenal.

We're not going to go into the specific mechanics of executing these shots. Working with your teaching pro is the best way to develop these shots, and the Internet or your local library have many instructional books and DVDs with detailed sequential photographs and video.

# KICK SERVE

You may already be using a kick serve, but probably not. The object of this serve is to give you a high margin of error over the net and a bounce that causes the ball to kick up and to the side. It takes a great deal of practice, but if you can develop it consistently, it is a great second serve. Not that consistent yet? Then try it as a change-of-pace first serve from time to time.

# SLICE SERVE

Again, the serve you are using now could be a slice serve. It is simply a serve hit with more sidespin than a conventional, flatter first serve. The slice serve is easier for most players to develop than the kick serve. The club player can often gain more confidence in the slice faster, and like the kick serve, it is a fine second serve or change-up first serve. Play with it, giving it more spin or less spin, but try to keep the same motion.

# TOPSPIN LOB

This is an amazing shot and amazingly difficult for the club level player to master. The idea is to lob the ball with so much top spin that it goes up and over the net player's head and the exaggerated top spin brings the ball right down into the court. Right. Fun to play with. Difficult to perfect.

# BACKHAND OVERHEAD

You probably want to do everything you can to avoid hitting a backhand overhead. It is an awkward shot. About the only time you're forced to hit one is when you're surprised by a low lob over your non-racquet shoulder. Have someone hit you a few while you're practicing. Remember to turn sideways

# APPROACH SHOT

This is a groundstroke that you follow to the net. The key here is to remember you are not trying to hit a winner. You are trying to hit a deep, quality shot that will put pressure on your opponent. Follow the path of your shot to cut down angle.

# HALF VOLLEY

This "hybrid" shot scares many players. It shouldn't. You just have to concentrate on taking the ball on a short hop. You've got to stay down with it and remember not to swing.

# DROP VOLLEY

The drop volley is simply hitting a drop shot from a volley. Taking the ball in the air and just dropping it over the net so your backcourt opponent can't get to it. This may be the one time your actual goal is to hit a winner, not force an error.

# PASSING SHOTS

When your opponents are approaching the net, DON'T try passing shots. Instead try to make them hit extremely difficult volleys. Make them bend, make them stretch, make them have to volley up, but leave yourself a larger margin of error than if you tried to pass them.

# SOME FOOD FOR THOUGHT

"The ideal attitude is to be physically loose
and mentally tight."
*–Arthur Ashe*

"Experience is a great advantage. The problem is that
when you get the experience, you're too damned old to
do anything about it."
*–Jimmy Connors*

"Ninety percent of my game is mental.
It is my concentration that has gotten me this far."
*–Chris Evert*

"You try to get the most out of what you are given, and
you have to enjoy the moment."
*–Pat Rafter*

"What is the single most important quality
in a tennis champion? I would have to say desire,
staying in there and winning matches
when you aren't playing that well."
*–John McEnroe*

"Success is a journey, not a destination. The doing is
often more important than the outcome."
*–Arthur Ashe*

"I love the winning. I can take the losing,
but most of all I love to play."
*–Boris Becker*

## CHAPTER 6

# PRACTICING FOR HUMANS

*"If I don't practice the way I should,
then I won't play the way
that I know I can."*
*–Ivan Lendl*

There can be little debate about the truth of Ivan Lendl's words about practice. In order to play your best tennis, you have to practice. There is no way around it.

Real human tennis players probably don't have the time or the energy or the inclination to practice as intensely as Lendl did. Nor do most club players really want to hit with a ball machine two hours a day or stop by the courts and hit serves every night after work or take a couple of lessons a week. Real humans are doing most of their practicing while they're playing. And that's fine!

If doctors can "practice" medicine and lawyers can "practice" law for their entire adult lives, then certainly tennis players should be allowed to practice tennis. In a very real sense, practicing is what you are doing each and every time you set foot on the tennis court. Whether you are just hitting for fun or playing an important match, what you are really doing is practicing tennis.

And in truth you can even practice when you're not on the court. You can practice from courtside, in your driveway, or even on the couch in the living room.

# PRACTICING AT HOME

You don't have time to go to the courts — you're waiting for Seinfeld reruns to start or the pasta to cook. You've got a few minutes to kill, so why not practice your tennis a little right at home. You don't even have to sweat if you don't want to.

**\* Hit against a wall, a rebound net, or even your garage door.** This is a fine form of practice away from the courts. The ball will bounce back too fast for you to practice your actual strokes, but a backboard is a great place to practice racquet control and footwork and touch. To make it more interesting, you can create targets, set goals of consecutive shots without a miss, or turn it into an aerobics session as well.

**\* Serve into a wall or an open garage or a fence or even a hedge.** Without the net and those lines to put pressure on you, you can relax and just concentrate on the service motion. Focus on the feel, the flow, the timing. It is not always important where it goes but more how it feels. Remember to hit up on the serve. And then remember to take "this serve" with you the next time you go to the court.

**\* Hit imaginary strokes.** Shadow tennis can often help you correct mechanical errors or help establish some good habits like getting prepared early. As in shadow boxing, shadow tennis is practicing your strokes and footwork and timing without a ball. Just imagine shots being hit to you and try to return them with form, grace, and timing. Be sure not to break any lamps with these great strokes.

**\* Go over different tennis patterns in your head.** As simple as it is, actually repeatedly "seeing" a serve-return combination, or a cross-court exchange, or perfect poaches in your mind's eye can transfer to the court. Talk about an easy way to practice!

## PRACTICING FROM COURTSIDE

Whether you are waiting to get on a court or cooling down courtside after a match, you can practice effectively while you're just sitting there watching. You don't even need a racquet.

**\* When you watch a singles or doubles match, try to "read one shot ahead."** Predict where a shot is going before it is hit, then where the return will go. You'll soon find out you are brilliant at this. Now apply this newly discovered "reading" brilliance the next time you are on the court.

**\* Concentrate on the most effective player in a foursome.** Try to figure out exactly why this person is the best. Is this person stronger or faster or smarter or simply more consistent? Don't get fooled. Often the player that looks the "best" at first is not the most effective player on the court.

**\* Study a few doubles teams.** Do some teams seem to cover the court more effectively and play better together than others? Do some teammates seem to be tripping over each other? Can you figure out what the differences are?

**\* Count how a dozen or so points end** in your head as you are watching. Chances are very good that this little counting exercise will remind you once again that tennis actually is a game of errors, not winners.

**\* Look for "yourself" in the players on the court.** Do you make some of the same errors, some of the same great shots?

# PRACTICING FROM YOUR COUCH

Certainly everyone can learn from watching the pros, but remember that the tennis you watch on television tonight has very little resemblance to the tennis you play on the court tomorrow. "Practicing" by watching the pros can get tricky.

Here are some suggestions of things you can watch for that all the pros do, and that the rest of us can and should do as well.

**\* Watch the pro's feet.** Every pro you will see on television starts moving before the ball is served and keeps the feet moving until the point is over. Small, quick steps. Every player!

**\* Notice their visual concentration.** The visual concentration of the pros is evident and intense. They start concentrating on the ball as soon as it is out of the can and don't "disconnect" until it is back in the can.

**\* Look at the positioning and anticipation.** The pros take an educated guess as to where their opponent's shot is going. Anticipating is something all the pros do. Yes, even the pros occasionally get caught zigging when they should have been zagging, but trying to anticipate more effectively will make you a better player.

The above are three examples of habits or skills the top pros have that humans should try to copy or incorporate into their own games. Next are a few things that the pros do that you should probably NOT try to copy or incorporate into your game. At least not yet.

* **Do not try to hit your first serve as hard** or your second serve with as much spin as the pros. First, because you can't, at least not with any consistency. Second, because you don't have to.

* **Don't try to hit your shots as close to the lines** or the net as the pros often do. Regular humans need a much, much safer margin of error both over the net and inside the court.

* **When you are in trouble, don't try to go for a winner.** Sometimes it is a pro's only hope, but you have safer, higher percentage options. Try a defensive lob.

* **Remember, the pros on television are exceptional athletes and extraordinary tennis players.** They have hit more tennis balls by age twenty than you'll hit by one hundred and twenty. They do this stuff for a living. You don't have to try to hit the way they do, and your opponents can't.

# PRACTICING ON THE COURT

Okay, you've practiced a bit on the backboard and you've studied some play from courtside, and you even "practiced" a little the last time you watched television tennis. But what really is the most fun and best practice is hitting with other humans.

One way to practice effectively when you're actually playing a set is to try to consciously practice only one or two aspects of your game. For example, concentrate on just varying your returns of serve or focus on your teamwork and your communication if you're playing doubles or maybe your approach shot if you're playing singles.

Concentrating and working on just one or two parts of your game at a time is generally more productive than simply going out on the court and "trying to play better." It goes back to setting simple, attainable goals.

You can also obviously practice on the court when you are not in a match situation. The possibilities are limitless, and the following are some suggestions to get you going.

**\* Serve and Return.** Simple. One person works on serves and the other returns. You do not play the points out. One person serves a dozen or so serves that his/her partner returns. Then switch. These are the two most important shots, and the two that people usually practice the least.

**\* Lob and Overhead.** One person starts at the net and puts the ball in play to the other person in the back court. You play out the points, but the only shots permitted are lobs and overheads. Play to ten points, then switch positions. This is a great workout and great practice for two underpracticed shots — the lob and overhead.

**\* Same-Team Tennis.** One player begins the "point" with a serve, and both players try to keep the ball in play with quality shots. You're on the same team trying to set a record for continuous hits without a miss. You can try for 20 or 2,000. You can also say all the shots must go crosscourt or behind the service line or whatever. The variations are limitless. The idea is to keep the ball in play.

**\* Ghost Doubles I.** In this game, the players are not using the singles court but playing diagonally on the doubles court. The server begins the point, and any ball that does not land in the half-doubles court on the diagonal is out.

**\* Ghost Doubles II.** The same as above except the point is not started with a serve. The ball is simply put in play. The point is played out in the doubles court, not on the diagonal but straight ahead. Yes, you get to use the alley.

\* **Mini-tennis.** The court is simply shrunk. The service line becomes the back out-of-bounds line. The serve is underhand and the ball can be hit on the bounce or in the air. You can't stroke the ball, but it can be excellent practice for your foot-work and racquet control.

It is all practice and it all really should be fun. So make up your own games, your own rules, your own ways of enjoying your "practice" time on the tennis court.

# FIVE IMPRACTICAL PRACTICING PRACTICES

*The following are only five examples of silly things you may have been guilty of when you thought you were practicing your tennis.*

**1.** Practicing mostly what you already do the best. Concentrating too much of your time on the aspects of your game that need the least practice.

**2.** Not practicing those things that you presently execute the worst. Avoiding working on the aspects of your game that need the most practice.

**3.** Practicing too long on shots or stuff you never plan to really use in a game.

**4.** Never really practicing at all. Just trying to win.

**5.** Forgetting to practice the two most important shots — the serve and return of serve.

# COACH, SOME STUFF IS STILL NOT WORKING

**"I'm trying to anticipate more but it seems every time I think left, they go right. I think short, they go deep. I'm a wreck!"**

Check to see if you are guessing wrong when you are simply watching and not playing in a match. Also, you may be anticipating and moving so early that your opponent has time to read the situation and still execute the shot. Also, see if a few fakes help.

**"Hey coach, I know what I should do, should have done, after the point is over."**

Good. This could be the opposite of the situation above. All you have to do is just take a chance and do it sooner.

**"Coach, I'm back. I did do the right thing earlier, but I missed the shot."**

Great! You figured out what to do and you figured out when to do it. Now all you need is some practice on executing the actual shot. That is the easy part. It really is.

**"I've read your book and now I'm thinking so much I can barely make contact with ball."**

Okay, put all this information in the "tennis locker" in the back of your brain and just pick one concept to deal with each time you play. Concentrate on just one thing at a time.

## CHAPTER 7

# USING THE ELEMENTS

*"It was so windy today I'm really glad I had a piece of chocolate cake last night to keep me from getting blown away out there."*
*–Maria Sharapova*

Sunshine, fresh air, a spring breeze — these elements may have been part of what first attracted you to tennis. These elements can still be your friends now that you are playing to win.

Most club level players won't be facing the blustery wind of the U.S. Open that Maria is describing above, but all of us have to deal with the elements — wind, sun, heat, cold.

The idea is not to let the elements be an excuse for losing but rather use them to your advantage in winning. The truth is that smart players often see the elements as an additional weapon for their arsenals. Here are several suggestions on how to get a little help from your friends.

# THE ELEMENTS IN GENERAL

* **Take a read on the elements during your warm-up.** Is the wind constant? Gusty? Strong? Is the sun going to be a factor? The temperature? Assess the situation quietly and carefully.

* **Plan how and when you can use your knowledge** and assessment of the elements to help you win the match or gain even a small advantage.

* **Try never to acknowledge the elements even exist** as either a positive or negative force. Outwardly, ignore their existence.

# THE POWER OF THE SUN

* **Always know where the sun is** and where it's going. Be aware of clouds and where they will be.

* **Use the sun and the clouds to help you.** If you can take an extra thirty seconds changing sides and start serving in the shade, why not?

* **Adjust your toss on the serve slightly** and you'll almost never have to "serve in the sun."

* **With the sun at your back, bring opponents to net** and lob at sun level. No, this isn't dirty tennis, it is smart tennis.

* **If an opponent's shot to you is going to be in the sun,** concentrate on the ball until it is about to pass in front of the sun, then let your radar go to work. Don't watch the ball into the sun.

* **Never acknowledge the sun,** never use it as an excuse, but use it wisely to help you win some of those big points.

## THE WIND

* **If the wind is gusty and unpredictable,** play safe shots with a larger margin of error. Keep balls lower, lob lower.

* **If you're playing into the wind, remember you can hit hard** on your ground strokes and lobs. Off-speed shots should be effective as well. Try to force your opponent to hit up on shots.

* **If the wind is at your back, slow down your swing** and exaggerate the follow-through. Remember you can't wait for balls to come to you. Move in more on shots, lob lower.

* **If the wind is blowing steadily across the court, use it** to help curve shots into the court or curve them into your opponent.

## THE TEMPERATURE

* **When it is unusually hot, consciously drink more water.** This is not only for your tennis game. It is for your health.

* **When the temperature is rising** you might want to shorten or lighten your pre-game warm up.

* **If shade exists anywhere, use it when possible**, during the changeover, in between points, whenever.

* **When it is unusually cold, layer your clothing** so as you warm up and then cool down you can add and subtract clothes.

* **Colder weather may call for a slower, longer warm-up process.** You don't want to begin actual play until you are warm.

# TENNIS FACT OR TENNIS FICTION?

### 1. Good players aim for the lines.
FICTION: Great professional players may aim for the lines, but human, club level players need a much bigger margin of error. Quite simply, if you are aiming for the lines too many balls will land out.

### 2. Usually the team or player with the highest percentage on returns of serves will win the match.
FACT: At the club level this is a fact that is illustrated in match after match. If you charted 100 matches, you would find the team with the most consistent return of serve would probably win over 90 of these matches. The other statistics wouldn't even matter.

### 3. Players make more errors on their backhand groundstrokes than their forehands.
FICTION: I know, I know, most people's backhands are not as effective as their forehands. But in a match we generally hit so many more forehands than backhands that we end up with more forehand errors. We probably have more forehand winners as well.

### 4. In doubles, a ball down the middle should be taken by the partner with the forehand.
FICTION: It's not a bad rule of thumb, but if you have a righty and lefty on a team there could be two forehands in the middle or no forehands in the middle. A better rule is the partner closest to the net has the choice on the ball down the middle.

# CHAPTER 8

# CHARTING AND SCOUTING

*"In these days of modern tennis,*
*a player is as strong*
*as his (or her) weakest stroke."*
*–Bill Tilden*

Bill Tilden uttered these words over a half century ago, but they are still true today. All players have weaknesses. If you can find them, you can exploit them. And if you can identify your own weaknesses, you can work to eliminate them or maybe hide them a bit.

Charting a match or scouting an opponent does not have to be a complicated process. This chapter offers some suggestions for charting matches to discover specifically how and why points and matches are won or lost, and also offers suggestions on scouting opponents and identifying their weaknesses and strengths.

# A CHART OF A MATCH

*Below is an example of charting a 3.5 doubles practice match. The chart indicates how each point ended: an "e" for error or "w" for winner in the appropriate box across from each player's name.*

|  | S | ROS | ROR | GS | V | OH | LOB |
|---|---|---|---|---|---|---|---|
| **Suzy** |  | w<br>w<br>e<br>e | w<br>e<br>w | e<br>e | e | e<br>e |  |
| **Betty** | e | w<br>e | e<br>e<br>e | w | w<br>w<br>e | w | e<br>e<br>e |
| **Lonni** | e | w<br>e | w<br>w<br>e<br>w | w | w<br>e | e | e |
| **Pat** |  | e<br>e<br>e<br>w | e<br>e<br>e | w | e<br>w<br>w<br>e |  |  |

KEY
S=serve, ROS=return of serve, ROR=return of return,
GS=groundstroke, V=volley, OH=overhead, LOB=lob

# READING THE CHART

Total points played: 50
Total errors: 31 (62%) Total winners: 19 (38%)
Points ended in first three shots: 27 (54%)
Points ended on serve: 2 double faults
Points ended on return of serve: 12 (7 errors, 5 winners)
Points ended on the return of return: 13 (8 errors, 5 winners)
Points ended on a volley: 10 (5 errors, 5 winners)
Points ended on overheads: 4 (3 errors, 1 winner)
Points ended on lobs: 4 (all errors, all lobbed long!)

# THE CHARTING PRO'S INTERPRETATION

*Half the points were won or lost on the return** and the return of the return. That means half of the points never really got started.

*As a group they tended to hit a shot and watch it** and then be surprised if it came back.

*The group tried to do too much with ground strokes** and tried to hit better shots than they needed to.

*The volleying was pretty good, but could have been better** had they moved a bit more.

### Some areas this group should work on:
*Stay up on the toes and anticipate shots** more. Try to think in two and three shot combinations, not one shot at a time.

*Don't go for too good a return,** even on weak serves.

*Be hungrier for volleys.** Anticipate rather than react.

*Lobs out are horrible errors.** One doesn't have to hit the lobs that deep, especially because the opponents' overheads are not very good. Never lob out. Make your opponents hit overheads.

# SCOUTING

Before you skip this section by saying, "Scouting? Get outta-town. I don't have time for that stuff" — stop. You don't have to follow your opponents around and hide behind the wind screens and furtively chart them.

Many times you already know your opponents. You can fill out a scouting report from memory and use it to make you more effective against that player. This is not official stuff with clipboards and computers; it's just some data that could help.

Be very careful not to be misled by what appear to be a player's strengths and weaknesses. You may realize that a player with a very strong forehand and fairly weak backhand actually makes many more errors on the stronger side.

| FRAN | 1 | 2 | 3 | 4 | 5 |
|---|---|---|---|---|---|
| patience | | | | X | |
| concentration | | | X | | |
| aggressiveness | | | X | | |
| consistency | | | X | | |
| anticipation | | | X | | |
| lateral movement | | | | X | |
| in/out movement | | X | | | |
| stamina | | X | | | |
| first serve | | | X | | |
| second serve | | X | | | |
| return of serve | | | | X | |
| forehand | | | | X | |
| backhand | | | X | | |
| lob | | | X | | |
| high volley | | | X | | |
| low volley | | X | | | |
| overhead | | X | | | |

## A SAMPLE SCOUTING REPORT
*(1= lowest, 5= highest)*

# A QUICK ANALYSIS OF THE SCOUTING REPORT ON PAGE 78

The strengths and weaknesses of this opponent seem fairly simple. The strengths are the ground strokes, lateral movement, return of serve, and patience. The weaknesses appear to be the second serve, moving into and back from the net, the overhead, and the volley. One obvious game plan against this opponent would be to try to move in and take advantage of the weak second serve, and also try to bring the opponent into net where movement, volleying, and the overhead are all weaknesses.

Below is a blank chart. You might try to fill it in objectively for your own game. It will tell you how smart opponents will plan to play you.

|                  | 1 | 2 | 3 | 4 | 5 |
|------------------|---|---|---|---|---|
| patience         |   |   |   |   |   |
| concentration    |   |   |   |   |   |
| aggressiveness   |   |   |   |   |   |
| consistency      |   |   |   |   |   |
| anticipation     |   |   |   |   |   |
| lateral movement |   |   |   |   |   |
| in/out movement  |   |   |   |   |   |
| stamina          |   |   |   |   |   |
| first serve      |   |   |   |   |   |
| second serve     |   |   |   |   |   |
| return of serve  |   |   |   |   |   |
| forehand         |   |   |   |   |   |
| backhand         |   |   |   |   |   |
| lob              |   |   |   |   |   |
| high volley      |   |   |   |   |   |
| low volley       |   |   |   |   |   |
| overhead         |   |   |   |   |   |

*(1= lowest, 5= highest)*

# "ALWAYS OBEY YOUR SUPERIORS, IF YOU HAVE ANY"

*That rather insouciant suggestion comes from Mark Twain. Following are a few more "always" suggestions.*

**ALWAYS** . . . take your time when serving. Develop a personal ritual (ball-bouncing, deep breaths, nodding your head) that enables you to relax and focus on your serve.

**ALWAYS** . . . start moving your feet before the server serves the ball. Bring the weight up on the balls of your feet and start to dance, rock, roll, bounce — whatever.

**ALWAYS** . . . move in at least one large step if your opponent faults on the first serve. Don't be subtle. Always be sure this "change of position" is noticed by the server.

**ALWAYS** . . . try to concentrate on the ball from the time it comes off your opponent's racquet until it hits your racquet. Look for the seams, the writing on the ball. Use any trick you can to increase your visual concentration on the ball. Try to watch each shot hit the strings on your racquet.

**ALWAYS** . . . get your racquet back early on your ground strokes. As soon as you know which side of your nose the ball is going to be on, start to turn in that direction and take your racquet back.

**ALWAYS** . . . chose the smarter, safer, higher-percentage shot over the flashy, highlight-film shot that makes the crowd go wild . . . the one time out of six that it goes in.

**ALWAYS** . . . stay with a winning strategy and almost always change a losing strategy. It is trite, but true.

**ALWAYS** . . . try to run down every ball, even if you don't think you can get there. You'll surprise yourself at some of your amazing impossible gets.

**ALWAYS** . . . play within your game, your capabilities. It is not likely that you will miraculously develop some new shot or skill in the middle of a match. You can't just decide to hit "better" shots, but you can decide to hit smarter shots.

**ALWAYS** . . . try to remember that "it is all practice" and that "it is only a game." Always try to keep your perspective, no matter what is happening on the court.

**ALWAYS** . . . play a ball as being "good" unless you are positive the entire ball landed outside of the line. If a ball is not unquestionably, positively, 100% "out," then it is unquestionably, positively 100% "in."

**ALWAYS** . . . bring a new can of balls to the court. You certainly don't have to volunteer to use them each time. You can decide to leave them in the car if you want to, but you'll know you'll always have new balls if no one else brings a can.

---

### *AND THREE MORE TO KEEP IN MIND*
"Always make water when you can."
*– Duke of Wellington*
"Always be a little kinder than necessary." – James Barrie
"Always remember that
criticism and praise are both frauds."
*– Unknown*

---

# COACH, I'M GETTING SMARTER AND PLAYING BETTER BUT . . . .

**"Coach, I've got two kids who are pretty good tennis players. Should I make them specialize in just tennis?"**

I don't think you should make them do anything. You can discuss the different options — the pros and cons of specializing in one sport. My two cents: The more sports the kids play, the better. Individual sports and team sports can offer different and equally valuable experiences for young people.

**"Coach, a friend of mine invited me to play on a grass court. I've never played on grass before. I'm afraid I'll make a fool of myself."**

If you are lucky enough to have the chance to play on grass, DO IT. You'll have to bend a little, try to hit a lot of shots before they bounce; but it is an experience you'll never forget. It's quieter, cooler; it's different, and it is fun.

**"Coach, I'm a 3.0 player and I want to change my one handed backhand to a two-hander so I can get a little more power. What do you think?"**

Tough to say. You would probably get a bit more power with both hands, but I don't know if that would make you a more effective player, Also remember that your footwork will have to be better. Play with it for a while before making any permanent decision.

# CHAPTER 9

## DEALING WITH DORKS

*"Everyone is calling me
a dork now."*
*–Maria Sharapova*

Ms. Sharapova's quote is referring to her mentioning that she collected stamps. Well, we don't feel this makes her a dork. Nor is this the type of dork we're talking about in this chapter.

We're talking about those tennis players who will do anything to win, from giving bad calls to denying touching the net to adjusting the score to not letting you warm up.

We have to deal with dorks in life and in tennis. Here are some suggestions for dealing with dorks on the tennis court.

# BAD CALLS

Everyone has had to deal with bad calls from time to time. Sometimes people want the ball to be out so badly that that's the way they see it. Other times people are purposely calling balls out that they know are in. Often these bad calls are planned for an especially important point.

The real key to dealing with the situation: Stay cool!

If an opponent calls one of your shots out that you felt was in, there isn't really much of an argument. It is your opponent's call and it is only one instance. If the call seemed especially "incorrect" you might quietly and politely ask if your opponent is sure of the call. No histrionics. No sarcasm — just a simple query. Whatever your opponent's answer, you accept it.

The reality is that if the ball is very close, your opponent is usually in a better position to actually see whether the ball landed in or out. Also, you are not exactly a disinterested viewer here.

If, however, this first questionable call is followed by what seem to be unquestionably bad calls, calmly and quietly stop play and request a lines person to call lines for the remainder of the match. It is no big deal, and if this option is available to you, the problem is solved.

If there is no provision for a person to call the lines, your options are somewhat limited. Your goal should be to play the match and live with the bad calls and, at the same time, not to let these calls destroy your concentration and your game. Most of the time the "bad caller" alone can't change the outcome of a match. The "bad caller" needs the "bad callee" to come unglued. So once again the answer is to stay cool and make it through the match.

If the calls become absurd and are unquestionably deliberate, you might want to make a statement of sorts. Select one of your opponent's shots, an obviously "in," easy-to-return ball — perhaps a second serve — and call it "out." Simply state, "I am calling that ball out." It is a little like judicial review. You're not saying it is actually out. You are saying you're calling it out. This "call" might get your point across, and maybe your opponent will begin calling the lines more fairly. Maybe not.

The above attempt at "judicial review" is a last-ditch effort to play the match by the rules. If the bad calls continue, it is useless and dishonest to simply copy your opponent's patterns of bad calls. You have two choices: You can default or you can just finish the match and stay cool. It's all just practice.

## NO CALLS

These are the calls that your opponents, according to the rules, have to make against themselves. Calls like touching the net, reaching over the net, whether your shot bounced twice before they got to it, and so forth.

Sure, you can remember those opponents who got to a shot so late it had stopped bouncing and was rolling, and yet they insisted they got the shot on the first bounce. It is their call. The key in these "no call" situations, in addition to staying cool, is **to keep playing the point** no matter how obvious the infraction. You play the point until it is over or your opponents make the calls upon themselves.

Even if a player hits the net with the racquet so hard that the net post vibrates, the point is still in progress until that player makes a call or the point actually ends with an error or winner. If you should win the point "anyway" the infraction does not matter. If you should lose the point, you can surely question your opponent politely. "I'm sorry, did you touch the net during that point, or was that an earthquake?" or "Are you sure that you got that shot on the first bounce?" But that is all you can do. Except, of course, be cool and don't let a "no call" or two affect your concentration.

Again, it is rare that one or two "no calls" in any match will determine who wins or loses.

# WRONG CALLS

Occasionally you may come across a dork who has decided it is easier to win games by making up the score rather than actually winning the points. The simple rule to foil this strategy is to have the server call out the score loud and clear before each and every point. If a server does not do this, then you do it for them.

Scoring sometimes seems the hardest part of the game. But whether a person is deliberately trying to "alter" the score or you are just getting mixed up, if everyone agrees on the score before the ball is served each time, the problem disappears. Make it a habit.

If you and your opponent(s) are honestly mixed up about the score and no one can reconstruct the points, then it is simply a time to compromise. It is a game of tennis and it's all practice.

# YOUR CALLS

Following is just a sampling of situations where an opponent may try to gain an advantage by being a bit of a dork. In these situations it is NOT their call, it is YOURS. Be cool. Be firm.

**The too short warm-up attempt.** Your opponents have been warming up for a few minutes. You arrive, step on the court and hit two forehands, and they say, "Okay, let's start."

NOPE. Just smile and explain you need to warm up and will let them know when you're ready to start.

**The between-match hustle.** You are playing a tournament. You just won a grueling three-set match. You walk off the court and your opponent for your next match says, "Good match. We're supposed to get started as soon as you get a drink of water."

NOPE. Smile and explain you're not really tired, but you're going to take a little rest. Make a phone call. Go to the gym for a short workout. Do some wind sprints.

**The "hard look" on your calls** or the questioning of your calls about which you are one hundred percent certain. Ignore the looks and politely and sincerely answer the "questions" with a verbal assurance, such as "The ball was out." Be cool. If you are sure, you are sure. End of story. And remember, if you are not absolutely sure the ball was out, then the ball was in.

**The always-late opponent.** We're not talking five or six minutes. Whether it is for fun or an organized team match or tournament, you do not have to waste your time. If it is a social game, simply don't ask this player again. If it is a tournament or match, there is a predetermined default time. You are in control and your time is important. Be reasonable but don't be a wimp.

Above are a few examples. A complete list might cover several pages. The general answer for dealing with dorks on the tennis court is the same as dealing with dorks off the tennis court.

Remain cool, calm, collected, and as "detached" as you can be from the dork's unpleasant antics. Remain polite and try not to let them get into your head.

Understand when you have control and when you don't. If you have no real control over the situation, just concentrate and practice your tennis. However, if you do have control, then exercise that control in a firm and friendly manner.

# MORE STUPID THINGS PEOPLE SAY

**"She doesn't do anything right. She has terrible form, but she always seems to win."**

If she "always seems to win" she must be doing a whole lot of things right. Check again. Also, remember there are no points awarded for "style" in tennis

**"We lost the match because of one service break in the third set."**

Probably not this simple. There were at the very least 20 other games in the match. The one service break in the third set may stick out in someone's mind, but it is not the only reason the match was lost.

**"The score was no indication of how close the match really was."**

The score is actually the definitive indication of how close the match was. What is meant above is that the game scores and the players' skills appeared to be closer than the final score indicates. Maybe that's not so stupid.

**"I can't believe I missed that. I used to own that shot."**

Yeah, a lot of people used to own 1970 Ford convertibles. They don't still own them, and they probably haven't owned them for much longer than it seems sometimes. It may have been a while since you "owned that shot." Maybe you never did.

# COACH, WE'VE GOT JUST A FEW MORE THINGS TO DISCUSS

**"It is easy to read this stuff, but it doesn't seem as easy to do."**

Of course it is easier to read it than do it. But actually putting the majority of these suggestions into practice should be easy, too.

**"You told me and my partner 'down the middle, down the middle, down the middle' but the other team gets them back."**

Yes. That's okay. When you hit shots down the middle in doubles, one of three things can happen: both opponents will go for the shot, neither opponent will go for the shot, or one opponent will go for the shot. The odds are definitely in your favor.

**"Coach, I understand that controlling the points wins matches. My problem is I can't control myself. I get tempted and hit too many dumb shots."**

This is good. This means you're human, so this book is for you. Everyone wants to go for a dumb shot once in a while. They're part of the fun. The key is to try to control the number of times you fall to these temptations. Don't quit cold turkey, just start cutting back a bit.

**"Coach, I can't even try to do one thing when I play."**

Okay, stop thinking. When you're on the court, try to just concentrate on the ball and moving your feet. See what happens.

# NINE SIMPLE NO-BRAINERS

*Here are nine simple no-brainers that could win you some cheap points.*

1. Move in noticeably after your opponent faults on a first serve, especially if a male human is serving.

2. Stand in a strange place to receive an important serve. Remember, you don't have to stay there.

3. Poach to the middle or fake a poach at least twice every game that your partner serves.

4. Hit the ball down the middle in doubles. If there is ANY question as to where to hit the ball, hit it in the middle.

5. Hit your first serve over the net. Don't ever fault into the net.

6. Talk more to your doubles partner. Call the balls earlier. Encourage and console each other. Communicate.

7. Remember it is easier to get "smarter" on the court than it is to get "better." Hit smart shots. Make smart mistakes.

8. Bring your brain with you to the court. If your mind is somewhere else — the office, home, doing errands, worrying about the kids, visiting the South Sea islands — then you might as well not be on the court.

9. Lob a ball now and then that you could have easily, effectively, and offensively driven. This "no-brainer" will win more than a few points for you.

# DON'T GET CAUGHT WITH YOUR . . . .

**Don't get caught** being carried away with your own brilliance. If you hit a few brilliant, low-percentage shots to win some points, don't start believing they'll work all the time.

**Don't get caught** protecting against a shot or situation that isn't going to happen. For instance, don't guard your alley if the ball has little chance of actually being hit there.

**Don't get caught** getting ahead of an opponent by using a certain strategy and then altering your strategy and playing "not to lose." If you've got a plan and it's working, then stick with it.

**Don't get caught** letting down in your brilliant comeback bid. The goal is not to come back and tie. The goal is to come back and win. If you are down five games to two, remember to take each game one at a time but plan to win five games in a row . . . not just three.

**Don't get caught** taking any lead for granted. Close out any game-set-match or you may become a victim of "pressure reversal syndrome." If you're ahead 5-1 in a set, the pressure is on your opponent not to lose. With each game your opponent wins, the amount of pressure shifts more to you and builds.

**Don't get caught** being unkind, ungracious, or unsportsmanlike after any match: win, lose, or draw.

# COACH, I'VE STILL GOT QUESTIONS

**"I'm getting my first serve in and following it to the net, but my first volley is sailing long."**

Congratulations on the first serve. Your transitional volley is probably sailing because you are hitting it on the run. Not taking that split step. It could be your volley is too flat. You might want to open the face of your racquet a bit.

**"You say ignore the elements. No offense, Coach, but how do I ignore 20-mile-per-hour gusts?"**

We didn't say "ignore." You're not supposed to let your opponent know the elements might be a problem for you. If you are aware of these wind gusts, you can play safer, lower lobs and give yourself a bigger margin for error on most of your shots.

**"I'm really nailing my overhead. Unfortunately these beautiful shots are ending up in the net."**

The most likely reason for the net getting in the way is that you are not turned sideways. Make sure your shoulders and hips are perpendicular to the net. You might also be making contact too far in front.

**"Working on all of these specialty shots is driving me crazy!"**

Simple. Don't work on the specialty shots. Forget about them. Just go out and play your game.

# CHAPTER 10

# WINNING MEN'S DOUBLES

*"The best men's doubles team*
*in the world is*
*John McEnroe and anybody else."*
*–Peter Fleming*

Peter Fleming was probably close to the truth when he said the above. Unfortunately, or perhaps fortunately, few human players have partners like John McEnroe.

In real life men's doubles can resemble a wonderfully choreographed exercise, a surgical air strike, or a bunch of guys hitting the ball very hard but not very often. Usually the latter.

Playing better men's doubles, winning more often, and having more fun is unquestionably a matter of brains, not brawn.

# THE GAME

Three basic, general, important reminders can help you.

**First,** men's doubles at the club level is not a power game. Crushing serves and monster ground strokes don't usually make winning teams. The truth is, in fact, that "power" is more often a reason for losing rather than winning a match. It remains a fact that the harder you hit the ball, the faster you swing your racquet, the more errors you will make.

**Second,** men's doubles matches, like most tennis matches, are decided by which team has the most errors, not which team has the most winners. The idea is not to "beat" the other team, but rather to get the other team to "beat" themselves. A goal is not to try to hit great winning shots but to give your opponents unlimited opportunities to hit "losing" shots.

**Third,** men's doubles victories go to the team that is in control. Your team must have a basic game plan. You must use your plan and your shots and your positioning to control your opponents, to limit their options. By controlling the patterns and flow of the points and by aggressively controlling the net, you will force more errors from your opponents and you will "win" the match.

# THE SERVER

Holding serve in men's doubles can be a perfect example of brains over brawn and effective team work.

The server's job is simple. Get your first serve in! Everybody knows this maxim, so why do so few first serves go in? Generally because the server hits the first serve too hard, and because the server tries to hit a better serve than he can actually hit with any consistency. Repeat: Get your first serve in!

Whatever it takes — less speed, more spin, less spin, or a safer clearance — get your first serve in. Every time that first serve goes in, it is a tactical and psychological lift for you and your partner. Every time that first serve is a fault, it is a lift and actual advantage for the receiving team. The receiving team becomes more focused on that second serve, more offense-minded, more confident.

After accomplishing the goal of getting your first serve in (almost) every time, your job is now to place the majority of these serves as close to the center line as you consistently can.

If you can hit a pretty good serve, deep and near the center line, you limit the receiver's choice and possible angle of his return. Your serve will actually be controlling where the return can go and your partner can be more aggressive at net.

The idea is not to have a handful of aces each match, but rather a truckload of consistent "pretty good" serves that enable you and your partner to control the play.

Obviously you don't want to try to hit every serve near that center line. Six or seven out of ten is probably a sensible number. So, what about the other serves? Following are some suggestions to keep your opponents off balance and actually make these "down-the-middle" first serves even more effective.

**\* Go for a zinger every once in a while.** Hit it harder than usual but not as hard as you can. Remember that the power comes from your legs, the shoulder turn, and rhythm. The power does not come from your arm. Think the ball over the lowest part of the net to the widest part of the court.

**\* Serve directly at the receiver.** Think it toward the non-racquet hip of the receiver (left hip for right-hander, right hip for left-hander). Don't try to serve any harder than usual, just directly at the receiver.

Remember you are not trying to win the point with your serve, but handcuffing the receiver can often force some weak returns.

* **Pull the receiver wide** with a slice and/or more angled serve. Although this serve "freezes" your partner (forces him to cover his alley), it can be a variation that forces an error and keeps the receiver from "cheating" too much on those serves to the middle.

* **Give your opponent a "change-up,"** an off-speed first serve. This slow ball can be especially effective against a "big hitter" or actually any receiver who is starting to get a rhythm on your serve.

## THE SERVER'S PARTNER

The job of the server's partner is to help the server win his service game. To do this the server's partner has to get into the brain of the receivers. He has to put pressure on the receivers to "get it by the net guy." He has to make the receivers look at him. His job is to tempt and torment the receivers, to frustrate and fool the receiver, to get the receivers to concentrate on him instead of the serve.

The server's partner's job is to have the receiver forget his goal of returning to the server and trying to beat the serving team and instead concentrate only on beating the guy at the net, the server's partner.

Sound like fun? Following are a number of suggestions to make your serving partner love you and the receiving team hate you.

* **Study the receiver** and learn how to read what returns he will be trying to hit off which serve. Many receivers "telegraph" what shot they are about to hit. Use this information.

* **Poach, anticipate, give head fakes,** stand in some preposterous position. Make sure everyone in the area knows you are there.

* **Challenge the receiver's ego.** Make him more interested in passing you down the line one out of three times than in putting the ball in play.

* **Make him try to hit the perfect lob** over your head that lands on the line. Make him want to hit the return so hard no one could volley it. Basically, force him into errors that are really "unnecessary"errors. Get inside his head.

* **Be active and be willing to look the fool.** If you are not passed and "embarrassed" two or three times a match you are not being active enough up there.

If the server does his job by getting a pretty good first serve in near the center, the server's partner should then be the one in charge — the player in control of the point.

# THE RECEIVER

The receiver's job or his goal is to return the serve over the net and in. It is not the goal of the receiver to hit a winner or "great" return. His job is to hit "boring" high-percentage returns usually back to the server — returns that put pressure on the server to make a shot.

If the server is following his serve to net, make him volley it. Make him bend and groan and have to put his own pace and direction on that first volley. Make him volley it up by keeping it at his shoelaces.

If the server is not following his serve to net, try to put the ball in play deep to the server and follow your return into the net.

The goal is not only to return the serve every time but to get it back early and to get it past (or, in the case of a lob, up over) the net man before he can react. The receiver's job is to have his returns neutralize the server's partner and keep pressure on the server.

The receiver's job is to hit the return back with boring cross-court shots six or seven times out of ten. And then to startle the opponents with completely different returns the other three or four times. Keep the opponents off guard.

* **Lift the ball up over the net man** with a motion similar to your cross-court drive. Go over the non-racquet shoulder of the server's partner. Your goal here is to force him to hit a difficult awkward shot and remind him he can't be leaning to the middle too often or hugging that net too closely.

* **Drive the ball directly at the net man** (server's partner). You're not trying to hit him and you are not trying to pass him down the alley. You are simply keeping him honest; reminding him, again, that he has to "stay home" more often.

* **Chip a short cross-court return** that forces a reluctant server to come into net. If it appears the server does not want to follow his serve to the net, there is probably a reason — he's tired, he can't volley, he's just more effective from the back court. Use this return to make the server move to where he doesn't want to be. Sort of a chip/dropshot hybrid.

* **Go low and slow with your return.** If the server is coming in a bit slowly, this will force him to volley up.

* **Throw up a cross-court lob.** If the server is coming in fast and tight, this safe return will slow him down a little. Remember that the lob is not only a defensive return.

* **Tempt the net man with a return.** If the server's partner is not volleying effectively, you might try to hit close enough to him so he has to try to volley it.

Use your different returns in combinations. Keep them guessing.

# THE RECEIVER'S PARTNER

The receiver's partner's job is to capitalize on his partner's good returns of serve . . . and to help bail his partner out on those not-so good returns.

His job description is very close to that of the server's partner. And in fact if his partner's return goes to the server in the back court, the job description becomes exactly the same.

In truth, if there is an effective return to the back court to the server, the teams in effect change positions and the receiver's partner should now be controlling where the serving team hits the next shot and perhaps be able to cut it off at the net.

# THE TEAM

Most players play doubles with many different partners. Obviously you and a partner are not always going to have similar skills or personalities or even a similar idea on how any match should be played. The only answer here is conversation and compromise. Both players need to discuss how to combine their skills and ideas and come up with a single team and strategy for any specific match. It is a tennis match, not the Super Bowl. If the "compromised strategy" seems less than perfect to you, give it a shot anyway.

If you are trying to create a doubles team that will play together as a team more often than occasionally, then you'll need to work together a little more closely.

**First,** try to make sure both teammates like each other on and off the court. Both players should share the same views on how important tennis is to the team. If one partner would prefer to win a Sunday morning match rather than the lottery, and the other partner doesn't care about either, this is probably not a good pairing.

**Second,** try to form a partnership in which the individual combinations of different skills, strengths, and weaknesses complement one another to form a solid team. Two solid, hard-hitting baseline-hugging singles players might not fit well together as a doubles team.

**Third,** both team members must agree on their overall philosophy and strategy in any given match. It does not mean the strategy or plan can't change, it just means both players have to be "on the same page" at any one time. The partnership will not work well if one partner is trying to beat the opponents with patience and the other partner is trying to beat them by hitting great winning shots.

No matter what the makeup of your team or your opponents, here are some suggestions that will help you work better together and win more often.

* **The key to minimizing confusion** is to be in good position as a team BEFORE your opponents hit a shot. After each shot your team hits, each partner should adjust court positioning accordingly.

* **Call any ball that is lobbed** by your opponents early, before the ball has crossed the net.

* **Remember it is better to make a "wrong" call too early** than a "right" call too late when deciding whose shot is whose.

* **On any drive hit by your opponents,** the player closer to the net (and ball) sees it earlier and has first choice. If he feels he can make an effective play on it, it is his. He must make his decision early and be decisive.

* **The partner who is farther from the net** (even if it is only a few feet) can see and react to his "closer" partner's move. The reverse is not true.

**\* Also, if there is a question as to whose shot it might be** in a quick or fast exchange of shots, the player who hit the previous shot is often more prepared to make the play on the next shot.

**\* The bottom line is that both partners agree** in theory on how to cover the court together as a team. If you have to fight your opponents and each other, victories will be scarce.

**\* On any given day it is unlikely that both members** of any doubles team are going to be playing their best tennis. Adjust your game plan a bit for the realities of the day. Cover for each other.

---

# A CASE STUDY

**The Situation:** Jimmy J. and Juan J. on the club team are good solid players. They win more than they lose, but seem to lose the close matches.

**The Problem:** After charting one of their close matches the problem became clear. Their returns of serve looked good at first glance, and although some of the returns were indeed impressive, one or two returns a game went into the net!

Even returns of second serves and non-forcing first serves were being missed. This is like starting each game behind by love-15 or love-30. In a close match this handicap was just too much to overcome.

**The Solution:** Concentrate on getting every return of serve over the net. Remember the return is not supposed to win the point. Practice returning to each other until each can hit twenty returns in a row over the net.

---

# DOUBLE TALK

*Some often-asked general questions about the game of doubles are answered below — no double talk.*

**Which court should I play?**

That would depend on you and your partner. The general rule is that the player with the best, most effective return of serve should play the ad court. There are of course other considerations, but that's a pretty good rule.

**If we're both at net how do we know whose ball is whose?**

The person closer to the net and closer to the ball has the choice (and probably the better shot), but you have to talk and make definite moves early, even wrong moves. Any ball that is lobbed should be called, no matter how "obvious" the call.

**My partner's a lefty. I'm a righty. Who should be where now?**

Since more balls come down the middle, it's nice to have both forehands there, but the "stronger return of serve" rule mentioned above probably supersedes this.

**My partner's return of serve is stronger. We are both righties, but I handle pressure and the big points better than my partner. Who should be where now?**

The pressure points are served to the ad court. If you're the pressure player, that should probably be your court.

**Who should serve first?**

A good answer here is let your opponents serve first. But if you mean who on your team should serve first, the answer has to be the partner who holds serve most consistently. This might not be the person with the best serve. Holding serve is a result of teamwork in doubles.

**My partner never comes to the net after serving. Should I play back when my partner serves?**

Probably not. You can still be effective and control many points from the net if your partner's serve is fairly effective. If, on the other hand, your opponents are taking control of the game and the net with almost every return of serve, you might have better luck playing back when this partner is serving.

**Where is the safest place to try to hit my overhead when I'm in trouble?**

Probably back down the middle deep or over your partner's head, so that the partner can cut off the next shot and give you a chance to reposition. In fact, that's not a bad answer for your overhead even if you're not in trouble.

**My partner gets furious when I make a mistake. I don't try to mess up, I just do sometimes. What should I do?**

That is an easy one. Don't play with that partner anymore. Life is too short.

# SOME JUNK FOOD FOR THOUGHT

"The conventional view serves to protect us from the painful job of thinking."

*–John Kenneth Galbraith*

"The serve was invented so the net could play."

*–Bill Cosby*

"Do I play tennis? Man, I had one of the baddest overhead rights of anyone. Bam."

*–Don King*

"She comes from a tennis-playing family. Her father is a dentist."

*–BBC2*

"I have avoided tennis for a long time because there was a great deal of pressure for me to play tennis. My dad played tennis." (Think he was a dentist?)

*–Brooke Shields*

"One of the many difficulties of mixed doubles is deciding which moving objects one wishes to keep an eye on."

*–Anonymous*

"The best way to make your (tennis) dreams come true is to wake up."

*–Paul Valery*

# COACH, WE GOTTA TALK

*"I tried lobbing 'safer' and to my opponents' back-hand to make them hit awkward shots, but they usually still get the ball back."*

Good. This means you are not lobbing the ball long anymore. They're supposed to get the ball back most of the time. Your lob is not supposed to be a winner. It is supposed to make the net person work, back up, stretch, hit a difficult shot, maybe force an error. Expect it to come back. It will often come back weak. Take advantage of this.

*"You told us our opponents would almost never BEAT us, that we would beat ourselves. Well, they hit a passing shot and a great overhead to win the last match."*

These last two winning shots may have ended the match. These two shots did not win the match. Probably you and your partner had more total errors than your opponents throughout the match. Or maybe you guys played smart, percentage tennis and they actually did beat you. It doesn't happen often.

*"Coach, I am getting passed down the alley when I poach."*

Good. That means your movement is controlling your opponent's return. It is okay to get passed. Next time try a few fakes to the center and cover the alley. You'll drive them nuts.

# TWO CASE STUDIES

## A CASE STUDY

**The Situation:** Debbie D. is getting her first serve in 100% of the time. She has "done what she has to do" to get the first serve in the court.

**The Problem:** Debbie has gone a bit overboard with this 100% stuff. She is basically floating in a short, weak first serve and the opponents are doing whatever they want with their returns of serve. Her doubles partners can no longer even get insurance.

**The Solution:** Let's get real here. The first serve has to have some spin, some speed, some depth and placement. If you have to lower your percentage from 100% to, let's say, 70% to hit a more effective serve, then that is what you have to do.

## ANOTHER CASE STUDY

**The Situation:** Brian M. can hit beautiful shots when he is playing with big hitters. He can match strokes with the most powerful players at the club. He can hit with the best.

**The Problem:** Yes, Brian can hit with the big hitters and better players, but when he plays against pushers or junkers or slicers and dicers, the quality of his shots tumbles.

**The Solution:** First he has to make an adjustment for these "special" opponents. They're not giving him any pace on their shots, so he has to move into these shots more, stay down with them, and follow through. He probably has to be a little more patient, think more of combinations of shots.

# CHAPTER 11

# POACHING MORE EFFECTIVELY

*"Many of the players famed for quickness on the court would finish dead last in a race of more than ten yards."*
*–Eugene Scott*

Most dictionaries offer a non-tennis definition for poaching as "trespassing on another's land to take something that does not belong to you." In tennis when you poach, it DOES belong to you and you are NOT trespassing.

The shot may have been headed for your "partner's side" of the court, but if you can cut it off effectively at the net, you definitely should. It is your shot. And as Gene Scott's quote suggests, you do not have to be exceptionally quick or fast or athletic to poach effectively. You simply need to use your head and feet.

The doubles team that controls the net will usually win. In fact, the team with the most effective poacher(s) will usually win. An active, effective, poaching net player can basically control where and how the opponents will hit their shots.

Try some of the stuff below and watch out. You'll become a monstrous point-winning machine at the net.

# POACHING TIPS

**\* You do not need to be especially quick or fast to be an effective poacher.** You have to pay attention to your opponent and to where the ball is coming from and where it is probably going.

**\* A good poacher does not even have to be a great volleyer to be effective.** By moving and cutting off angles, the poacher can force the opponents into hitting lower percentage, more difficult shots, and can thus force them to commit more errors.

**\* Most often, an effective poacher is not "sneaking" over to cut off shots, not always trying to surprise the opponent.** The stealth poach can be an effective move occasionally; most of the time you want the opponent to see or sense your "move."

**\* Speaking of "fakes," they can be very powerful, controlling weapons.** Against certain players a lean or nod or step toward the middle can guarantee a shot down your alley. Hmmhhh.

**\* The choreography of a strong poach is a lateral move and then a step into the ball** — a move parallel with the net to get into position and then a shift of your weight in toward the ball.

**\* If you decide to try and poach more, you will be "punished" and look a little foolish occasionally.** You are experimenting with some new tactics. When you become a great poacher, you will also be "punished" and look a little foolish occasionally. That is okay because for every time you look "foolish" and "give away" one point, you will probably win five other points.

**\* Deciding to poach or cut off a shot after it has been hit is often too late.** If you were not thinking about cutting it off before it was hit, you should probably let your partner play the shot.

**\* Never apologize for those frame-rattling winners that carom off your racquet when you cut a ball off.** You were smart enough to be in the right place to make the play. You deserve the point.

**\* Direct your poached volley** where it will be effective — angled into the open court, at the feet of an opponent, or deep right down the middle.

**\* If your partner feels the tennis court is divided** down the middle line and balls that would land on one side belong to one partner and balls that would land on the other side belong to the other partner, get a new partner.

---

# A CASE STUDY

**The Situation**: Paula C. and Pam P. are both good volleyers and good poachers and both are very aggressive at the net.

**The Problem:** When both partners end up next to each other at the net, and a ball is hit down the middle, they both go for the shot and almost hospitalize each other.

**The Solution:** Never be "next to each other" at the net. One partner should always be a bit behind the other. The "closer" partner takes the shots down the middle

---

# "OCCASIONALLY, IT'S ALL RIGHT LETTING YOURSELF GO,

## AS LONG AS YOU CAN LET YOURSELF BACK"

*Thank you Mick Jagger. Following are some other "occasionallys" for on and off the court.*

**OCCASIONALLY** . . . hit your second serve first and your first serve second. The former is like a baseball pitcher's "change-up" and the latter (whether or not it goes in) may keep your opponent from always moving in on your second serve.

**OCCASIONALLY** . . . start out in a preposterous place to return serve — "too close," way "too far" right or left. Challenge the server. (Remember you don't have to stay where you "start out.")

**OCCASIONALLY** . . . drive a hard return of serve down the alley close to the server's partner. It is a low-percentage shot, but (whether or not it goes in) it may send a message.

**OCCASIONALLY** . . . when playing the net, fake a move to the middle and wait for the alley shot. You'll surprise yourself by how much influence you have over where your opponent tries to hit the ball.

**OCCASIONALLY** . . . very occasionally, try to hit a highlight-film winner when you're on the run or in trouble. It

110

is a dumb shot, but the "occasional" times you make it will feel wonderful.

**OCCASIONALLY** . . . for an entire set concentrate on hitting every shot down the middle — serves, strokes, drop shots, lobs. Down the middle. Down the middle.

**OCCASIONALLY** . . . when playing doubles, plan to use the "Australian Formation" when your team is serving. If you are lucky, it will confuse your opponents more than it confuses you.

**OCCASIONALLY** . . . experiment with different spins on a shot. You don't have to be a "tennis vegematic." Just add some topspin to a forehand or a bit more underspin to a backhand, or maybe slice the serve more than usual.

**OCCASIONALLY** . . . try to spend an entire match hitting no "winners." Hit good shots, but instead of "trying" to win, simply try to control each point, try to control the tempo and pace of each game.

**OCCASIONALLY** . . . ask a player who is not as good as you are — a player with less experience and skill — to hit some balls or play a set or two. (If the reverse has ever happened to you, you'll understand why.)

> ### HERE ARE SOME OTHER "OCCASIONALLYS" TO THINK ABOUT
> "Occasionally look out for number one and
> always be careful not to step in number two."
> – *Rodney Dangerfield*
> *(perhaps rephrasing Harry Truman)*
> "Occasionally the growth of wisdom may be gauged
> exactly by diminution of ill temper."
> – *Nietzsche*

# WIN THREE POINTS, WIN THE SET

*That's right. You probably only have to win three "big points" to win most sets. If both teams or players are evenly matched, the team that wins these big points will usually win. For instance, in the 2007 Gentlemen's Wimbledon five-set finals, the winner, Roger Federer, won only seven more points than Rafael Nadal, the runner-up. Only seven more big points in five sets!*

**What are these big points?**

> \* Obviously a set point is the biggest.

> \* A game point at 3 - 1 is a big point.

> \* A game point at 4 - 3 can be a big point.

> \* Your game point if you have lost two games in a row and were down love forty in this game could be a very big point.

**Big points appear in many, many different situations in many different matches. So, how do you win these three points?**

**First, you have to be able to identify these big points.**

**Second, you have to have a plan in mind.**

**Third, you have to play these big points with a heightened concentration and intensity.**

**And fourth, you have to execute.**

# CHAPTER 12

# WINNING WOMEN'S DOUBLES

*"Behind every tennis player*
*there is another tennis player."*
*–John McPhee*

John McPhee wasn't actually describing a doubles team, but he well could have been. Whether it is men's or women's doubles, it is about teamwork. Tennis is tennis. Doubles is doubles. But at the club level men's and women's doubles are often composed of different patterns and opportunities for improvements.

So, both chapters are included in this book and treated somewhat differently. The bottom line is, if you play doubles, you should look at both chapters. Each chapter touches on common areas of opportunity for everyone, men or women.

# THE GAME

Up to a certain level in women's doubles (and men's, too) the team with the stronger, more consistent forehand ground strokes is the team that prevails. The game consists mostly of cross-court ground strokes with an error on one of these shots usually ending the point. The serve is not really a factor, overheads are rare, and net play is a minor factor at best.

The points in one of these games can often resemble a ghost doubles game with two observers. There is nothing wrong with this level or these patterns of play. The players are having fun, competing, and getting exercise. However, by expanding their games a little, by experimenting and changing these patterns, all four players could be more involved, have more fun, play on a higher competitive level, and develop their net play.

At this next level of play, the team that plays the net more often and more aggressively becomes the winning team. The ground strokes are still important, but the team that controls the net controls the play.

This does not mean the server must follow her serve to net or that both players should be at net most of the time. It simply means that an effective net player can control where her opponents try to hit their shots. If a team (or even one player on a team) can do this, that team will win more often and the game will become more interesting and more complex.

# THE SERVER

The serve generally is not as much of a factor in women's doubles as it could be. There are exceptions, but generally there aren't many double faults or offensive, consistent first serves.

All too often the serve just puts the ball in play.

There is no reason why you can't make your serve a more effective weapon fairly easily. You probably don't have to change your service motion or hit a "better" serve. You can actually develop a more effective serve with your brain and a little confidence-building practice. Very seriously, you really can think your way to a more effective serve.

**\* Watch the ball until you hit it.** Never fault into the net. Get your serve over the net. Always.

**\* Have a target in mind every single time you serve,** first or second serve. It doesn't even matter if the ball goes there. Have a target in mind every time you serve. Directly at the receiver, down the center line or wide to the side, have a target in mind.

**\* Target the majority of your serves to land near the center line.** Remember, where your serve lands has much to do with where it will come back.

**\* Think of your serve and your team's next shot as a "one-two punch."** In fact, start trying to think of all your shots as two- and three-shot combinations.

**\* Read your opponent.** Where does she line up to receive the serve? Is she trying hard to protect a weakness? Does she move well? How can you keep her off balance?

**\* Make the receiving team return to your strength.** Through your and your partner's positioning and placement of your serve you can actually make the other team return to your strengths. A ball hit down the middle often comes back down the middle.

**\* Remember you can improve your serving effectiveness** with some teamwork, a little practice, and a mind set. Work together as a team to improve each other's serves.

# THE SERVER'S PARTNER

In any doubles match (men, women, mixed) it is the job of the server's partner to help win that game. The server's partner has to become a factor in the receiver's mind. She should try to intimidate and control the receiving team.

Too often too many players have been taught that "protecting the alley" is the server's partner's most important job. It most definitely is not.

It is rare that any team loses a match because a receiver continually hits effective shots down the alley. It is not rare that a server's partner religiously protects the alley and almost never gets to hit a volley.

**\* Be active up at the net.** Poach. Stand back a few steps or over a few steps to tempt the receiver to hit where you actually want her to. Give a head fake every once in a while.

Yes, you will miss some shots. Yes, you will now be passed down your alley (occasionally) and yes, you will look and feel like a jackass from time to time. It's okay.

**\* Force more errors.** That is what you will be doing as your reading and moving and poaching become more effective. And they will become more effective the more you try them.

**\* Get into the game.** If you are standing and never hitting it is your fault. "They don't hit it close to me" is no excuse. Nor is "I couldn't reach THAT." You could have if you had moved earlier.

**\* Remember that when you make a move to the center** and the receiver hits a strong shot that goes into the top of the net or just wide, she did not "have" you. Quite the contrary, you just had her. You won the point without even having to hit the volley.

# THE RECEIVER

If the server's partner is guarding the alley, the receiver's job is easy. Try to hit, early, a safe high-percentage shot back to the server. If the server has to serve and play a shot that comes right back at her all match long, that's a lot of work and pressure for her.

If, on the other hand, the server's partner is active and effective at the net, the receiver's job becomes a bit more complicated. You still want to return the serve to the server as much as possible, but now you'll have to freeze the partner. Keep her honest and guessing where you are going to return. A couple of low lobs over the net person's non-racquet shoulder might be useful.

You are really playing chess with the server's partner as much as or more than with the server herself in this situation.

Here are a few ideas to add spice to, if not your life, at least your returns of serve. Have fun with them.

* **Decide what shot you're going to try to hit** before the ball is served. Don't pay any attention to how the net person moves. Keep your eye on the important moving object, the ball.

* **Watch the ball until you have hit it.** Don't get fooled by this other moving object, the server's partner.

* **Return smart.** A crisp, well-hit cross-court forehand that bounces near the service line and goes to the server's forehand is a common return. Although this is an example of a good "stroke," it may not be an especially smart "shot." You generally do not want to return to a team's strength.

* **Hit where they used to be.** If the person at net is always moving somewhere, hit where they were last.

**\* Use the short, soft cross-court return** to make the server come in who may not want to come in. This will also cause some confusion.

**\* Hit close to the net person who doesn't seem to want** to volley. If the net person is not happy there, you may be able to force some errors or cause, again, some confusion.

**\* Hit lobs on returns you do not have to lob.** In other words sometimes lob a ball that could have easily been driven. Maybe try one game with only lob returns. Shake 'em up.

## THE RECEIVER'S PARTNER

The receiver's partner's job is obviously to help the team break serve, but her job can change greatly depending on the opponents in a given match.

**\* Play in tight to the net** if the server and her partner are both playing back or if you are confident your partner can get her return past the server's net-playing partner.

**\* Play at about the service line** if you are uncertain whether your partner can pass the net person. Move in if she does and defend yourself if she doesn't.

**\* Start all the way back at the baseline** if the serve is consistently stronger than your partner's return. It is the least effective formation but sometimes the safest.

## THE TEAM

If the individuals on a team are too polite or too deferential, it can definitely hurt the team. Talk to each other before, during, and after matches. Put your heads together to decide your team's strategy and how you will best complement each other's play.

**\* Remember that the court is not divided into your side, my side.**

**\* Call every lob hit by your opponents.** Call early, before it is on your side of the net. Call every single lob.

**\* Give yourself a break.** It is sometimes easier to accept or excuse our partner's errors and not our own. Everybody is allowed to make mistakes because everybody is just practicing.

**\* Talk to each other.** During side switches talk, take a read on what is happening, encourage each other, adjust your game plan, just bond a bit.

**\* Arrive at the court a little early,** together if possible. Put on your game faces together, adjust to a tennis frame of mind.

---

# A CASE STUDY

**The Situation:** Mary Beth F. and Jennifer H., a solid doubles team, played well together and were great front runners, but if they fell behind by more than a game they just seemed to come apart.

**The Problem:** Both players felt pressure to hit winners even if only one game behind. The result was quite predictable. Both made a much larger number of errors and the close match turned into a one-sided loss.

**The Solution:** If the team is in a close match and executing well and has a good game plan, they can still fall behind by a game or two or even three and have no reason to change anything they are doing. There is no reason for panic. Stay with a good game plan and hang in there.

---

# COACH, CAN WE TALK SOME MORE?

**"Coach, I'm a good volleyer so no one ever hits shots anywhere near me at net."**

Then move so they have to hit it near you or out. Be more active. Move around. Tempt them to pass you.

**"Coach, you keep saying 'it is all practice.' Well, it is not all practice. I also play team matches and tournaments."**

It has to do with your perspective. When you are playing a match or a tournament you are certainly trying to play your best and win, but isn't it also practice and experience for your next match or tournament?

**"Coach, you say just stay cool when some opponent is cheating you. That's not easy to do."**

No one said it was easy. It isn't, but it is probably the best way to deal with these situations. If you lose your cool, you'll lose your focus, and the dork will have made you beat yourself.

**"Coach, I love this game, but I'm just not as good as most of my friends."**

So what? That gives you more room for improvement. The real statement is "you love this game." That's what counts.

120

# TRUE OR FALSE #2

*Following is another test. The answers are on the next page, and, as before, do what you want here.*

**1. True or False?** The serve is definitely the most important shot in the game.

**2. True or False?** In doubles, generally, the most effective serve is to the backhand of either receiving opponent.

**3. True or False?** At net, anticipation and "court sense" can be more important than the actual mechanics of the volley.

**4. True or False?** The best way to "neutralize" an effective poacher is to try a hard, winning return down the line.

**5. True or False?** When "lobbing" an opponent who is at the net, one should try to hit the ball over the net player's head so that it lands within two feet of the base line.

**6. True or False?** Those doubles teams that win the most do so because, as a team, they have no real weaknesses.

**7. True or False?** If you are playing on a soft court (clay or Hartru) and someone can point to an actual ball mark on the court behind the line, this proves the ball was out.

**8. True or False?** In most matches the number of errors is slightly higher than the number of winners.

**9. True or False?** When extreme conditions occur like wind, sun, heat, cold, mist, you can actually use these conditions to help you win.

# ANSWERS

**1. FALSE.** A very convincing argument can be made that the return of serve is the most important.

**2. FALSE.** The best place to serve the majority of your serves in doubles is down the middle. This strategy limits the opponent's choice and angle of return.

**3. TRUE.** The net player who moves and anticipates will probably be more effective than the player who hits beautiful volleys if the ball comes right to them.

**4. FALSE.** The best, smartest, safest way to neutralize a good poacher is to hit a boring, offensive lob up over the outside shoulder. A hard winner is too often a loser.

**5. FALSE AGAIN.** A simple explanation is that if anyone tries to hit any shot within three feet of any line, it will go out too often. You need a bigger margin of error.

**6. FALSE.** All teams have relative weaknesses. Winning teams protect or minimize the exposure of their weaknesses and get maximum effect from their strengths.

**7. FALSE.** Certain shots (low, hard shots; shots with a lot of underspin) can actually hit the tape and be definitely "in" and yet still skid and leave a mark behind the line.

**8. FALSE.** The ratio of "errors" to "winners" in an average match is probably about seven errors for every three winners (7:3).

**9. TRUE.** "Adverse" conditions like sun, wind, and even mist, can be advantages that can actually help you. You have to adjust to the conditions and learn how to use them to help you win.

# CHAPTER 13

# SURVIVING MIXED DOUBLES

*"An otherwise happily married couple may turn a mixed doubles game into a scene from 'Who's Afraid of Virginia Woolf.'"*
*–Rod Laver*

Mixed doubles can be a classic competition. It can be a precision pairing of two individuals who have become a single tennis machine. Or as Rod Laver suggests above, it can be a divorce lawyer's dream come true.

For the purposes of this chapter we are dividing mixed doubles into two different and distinct activities: Competitive Mixed Doubles and Social Mixed Doubles. This happens also to be the safest way to make the division of these very different activities in real life. Keep in mind that tennis is only a game and it's all practice.

# COMPETITIVE MIXED DOUBLES

In competitive mixed doubles you and your partner have signed up together to compete in an organized competition like a tournament or team match. The assumption is that you are both of relatively sound body and mind and that you understand that each team in the competition will be trying to beat you any way they can.

There is no magical strategy for mixed doubles. Since it is merely a hybrid of men's or women's doubles, rereading those chapters and any doubles special features may help you to survive. Good luck.

# SOCIAL MIXED DOUBLES

Social mixed doubles comprises the rest of the mixed doubles played. For most humans this represents the much larger percentage of their mixed doubles tennis activities. Because a great deal of social mixed doubles is enjoyed by teams who are couples off the court and because most couples don't choose their mates according to their court prowess, the differences in skill levels of the four players on the court can be vast.

So, social mixed doubles is a different animal. The goal here is for everyone to have fun, hit some shots, run around, get some exercise, and have a few laughs.

Everyone will enjoy it more if all four players remember that the idea in social mixed doubles is not winning or exploiting your opponents' weaknesses. It is not a competition; it is a vehicle to socialize, get some exercise, and have some fun.

Certainly, if you have a foursome that is quite evenly matched you can have a competition of sorts within the social structure. But it is the social aspect rather than the competitive aspect of this game that must rule on these occasions.

# A HANDFUL OF THINGS TO DO

**\* Do tone down the speed of your shots and level of play a bit** if you are stronger than the others on the court. Do this subtly, rather like doing a good deed that will never be discovered.

**\* Do feed some easier shots to an exceptionally weak player.** They will gain some confidence and start to play better and everyone will have more fun and that is what it's all about.

**\* Do play like the points in "same-team tennis"** in the chapter on practicing in this book. Keep the ball in play.

**\* Do your best to keep the ball in play if you are one of the weaker players** on the court. You don't have to try for winners or be any better than you are. Just play it safe.

**\* Do even teams off as best you can if a set has been one-sided.** Try to pair teams so it is the most fun for everyone.

# AND A HANDFUL NOT TO DO

**\* Don't take advantage of an obviously weaker opponent.** Winning is not the thing here. Perhaps play to the stronger player.

**\* Don't try to put the ball away or try for winners.**

**\* Don't hit the ball any harder than the weakest person** on the court can handle comfortably.

**\* Don't apologize every time you make a mistake or error.** It's all practice and everybody makes mistakes.

**\* Don't instruct a weaker or less experienced player** during play, even if they ask you to. You can help, but don't instruct.

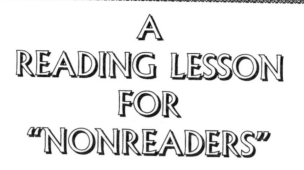

# A READING LESSON FOR "NONREADERS"

*All through this book there are references to "reading" your opponent, anticipating where the ball will be hit. Some players simply dismiss or ignore these suggestions by explaining, "I have enough trouble just hitting the ball back twice in a row."*

*Well, hitting the ball back twice or twenty times in a row is easier if you know where the ball will be.*

*Reading what an opponent is going to do isn't very difficult. You can read the player, the personality, or the percentages.*

### READ THE PLAYER

Most club-level players are very readable. Pay attention to where they're hitting from and be sure to watch their racquets closely.

Most players also hit certain shots back to the same place fairly consistently. It may be different places for different players, but the individuals are usually fairly consistent.

Many players telegraph their lobs. They prepare differently for the lob than for a drive. It's an easy read.

### READ THE PERSONALITY

The player who wants to beat you and to hit winners is very readable even with your eyes closed. If you appear to give these opponents what looks like room to hit a winner to your right, then that is where they'll try to hit it.

The aggressive, offensive player will usually be more aggressive and take more chances when winning and fewer when things are even or they are behind.

The player who doesn't want to make mistakes will try to hit the safest shot available in any situation.

The player with the big serve can be challenged simply by your body language and positioning for the return.

## PLAY THE PERCENTAGES

Most players have more confidence in their forehands, and they will drive their forehands if they have the chance.

The corollary is most players lack confidence in their backhands.

Most players prefer to hit their ground strokes cross-court.

Most players' second serves are noticeably weaker than the first.

So, you can read your opponents' bodies and you can read their minds. You can also simply play the percentages.

Most players are predictable as well as readable. If you are paying attention, you will know where they are hitting their shots. You can raise your level of play. You will have more time to cover the court effectively. You will be able to prepare earlier. You will execute more smoothly.

Not a bad reward for just doing a little reading.

# MORE, MORE, MORE!

*Move your feet more, stay up on your toes more.*

*Take more steps – quick, small steps.*

*Anticipate more; guess where and how a shot will be returned.*

*Move in more toward the net when volleying; step in more.*

*Concentrate visually on the ball more than you do, much more.*

*Poach more.*

*Fake poaching more.*

*Plan more, devise a strategy and method for each match (alter it if you wish, but plan more).*

*Talk to your doubles partner more.*

*Get more first serves in – do whatever it takes.*

*Take more lessons.*

*Practice more.*

*Laugh more on the court.*

*Have more fun.*

# CHAPTER 14

# PLAYING BETTER SINGLES

*"It's one-on-one out there, man.*
*There ain't no hiding.*
*I can't pass the ball."*
*–Pete Sampras*

Pete Sampras hit the nail on the head! Singles. A great contest. One against one. No alleys. No partners. No excuses.

The singles chapter is going to change focus from the other competitive chapters just a bit. Instead of focusing directly on you, the focus will now switch to your opponents; first to very specific types of opponents, then to opponents in general, and finally to that mythical opponent — the short ball.

Each time you walk on the court for a singles match, you have your arsenal of weapons with you. You have your strengths and your weaknesses and a certain style of play that works best for you.

Try to change the focus here from you to your various opponents. Often, winning more tennis matches has a lot to do with helping different opponents beat themselves. First, let's look at some very specific types of opponents.

**The Movers.** These opponents can move like the wind, seem never to get tired, and run down virtually every shot. These players are used to hitting on the move and taking advantage of angles, and their quickness, and their speed.

Take these advantages away from them. Don't make them move. Hit everything right to them down the middle. They can't use their superior speed to any advantage, and you've taken their angles for their shot-making skills. Many Movers will be less effective and make more errors when they aren't forced to move.

**The Pushers.** They just hit consistent shots from the back court with no pace or angles. It is often hard to do anything offensive with these paceless shots. Pushers seem to be trying to bore you into errors or maybe tears.

Pushers are usually happier in the back court, so make them come to net by hitting a short ball. Go to net yourself and put some pressure on them to win some points. Move in on your ground strokes. Hit them early to try to throw off the Pusher's timing and add a little more pressure. Get them to rush some shots.

**The Big Hitters.** They are out there to hit winners, big shots like on television. They want to overpower you. They are intimidating and can draw you into trying to outhit them. They can sucker you into trying to match their power with power. It is much easier just to use their power against them.

Just block the big hitters' shots back to them. Use their speed. Don't try to match power with power. Give the big hitters as many opportunities as possible to overhit. Tempt them with low percentage opportunities. And remember, big hitters can make big errors even on weak returns.

**The Junkers.** These players are often close cousins of the Pusher. The Junkers have an assortment of ugly-looking strokes. Their shots spin and sink and float and bounce funny. They seem to be impossible to return with good shots. They can destroy your rhythm and cause your game to unravel.

Increase your visual concentration, because the ball may be moving or bouncing differently. Next, try to move in and hit the shots a little earlier. Return them sooner to these opponents to rush them a bit. Keep your feet moving so you can adjust to surprises. Don't try to out-junk a Junker.

These are four general examples of different opponents. The point is that you have to take your opponent's style into consideration when you are devising a game plan. You certainly can't decide to change your skills for a given match, and you probably can't just change your style of play drastically, but you can adjust your strategy.

You can play your game, your style, but you might employ slight differences — a bit of fine tuning — depending on whom you are playing against.

Here are some ideas to keep in mind no matter what type of opponent you are facing.

**\* If your opponent has an easy put-away shot** and can hit it literally anywhere on the court, make a move in one direction (take away one part of the court) just before your opponent hits the shot.

\* **If you have put your opponent way out of position** wide, occasionally hit back to where the opponent was rather than into open court.

\* **If early in a match you are playing well** and fairly even with your opponent, but you are losing because this opponent is hitting some truly amazing winners, relax and keep playing the way you are. Your opponent will either have to continue to beat you with great shots, or the percentages will catch up. You'll be fine.

\* **If you have to move more than two steps laterally** to get to a strong serve, hit a safe, slow return. Just try to block the ball back as safely and effectively as you can.

\* **If your opponent is doing a great job of digging low** volleys out time after time, make them hit higher volleys. Try aiming for the right armpit (left armpit for lefties). This is often an awkward location for even very effective volleyers.

\* **If you think you are in for a long, even match** and you know you have a conditioning advantage, use this knowledge. You might risk a few points, or even games, early to make your opponent have to expend a great deal of energy. Conditioning is part of the game. If you can wear your opponent out, do it.

\* **If any of your shots land deep** in your opponent's court, they are good shots. It doesn't matter how they got there.

\* **If your opponent is having the best day ever,** try to bring them back to reality by making them hit as many shots as you can. If you can keep them hitting, maybe they'll fall back to earth.

\* **If, on the other hand, you are the one in the zone** and playing magnificent tennis, don't think, don't try to analyze, don't do anything. Just follow your bliss.

# SINGLES AND THE SHORT BALL MYTH

**THE MYTH.** *In singles you are hitting ground strokes, hoping to force your opponent to hit a short ball so you can move in and put away the shot.*

**THE REALITY.** *When you force your opponent to hit a ball that comes back short:*
   *1. The ten or twelve feet you move in to hit the shot "shortens the court" by ten or twelve feet.*
   *2. As you move closer to the net, it gets "higher" and becomes more of a barrier, relatively speaking.*
   *3. You are hitting a ball on the move. The ball is moving toward you, you are moving toward the ball.*
   *4. If you don't put this ball away, you have to either move in or move back. Otherwise you'll be mired in no-person's land.*

*The truth is that the short ball is not an automatic advantage, but you should still be able to capitalize on these short balls and win many points. Practice and pay attention.*

* **Anticipate the short ball.** Read when it is coming so you can move in early and not have to scramble to get there.

* **Turn your shoulders** and take your racquet back as you are moving in and long before you are going to hit the shot.

* **Shorten your backswing a little,** but be sure to follow through and keep the strings on the ball.

* **Try to execute a solid, boring, safe, deep shot.** Do not try to hit a winner.

* **Move in after you hit,** following the direction of your shot. Be prepared to play the next shot on the fly, as early as possible.

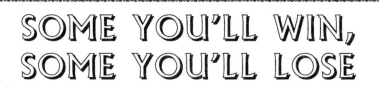

# SOME YOU'LL WIN, SOME YOU'LL LOSE

*There are times when you walk on the court to play a match and the winner can reliably be predicted. You are either much more effective than your opponent or your opponent is much more effective than you are. There are stunning upsets every once in a while. "David beats Goliath 0-6, 6-4, 15-13." The exception proves the rule.*

*If you find yourself on either side of a significant mismatch, you still have choices and you still can be in control.*

## IF YOU CAN'T LOSE, WIN SMART

You are significantly more effective than your opponent. You are the much better player and having one of those days when your mind is working like Einstein, your feet moving like a tap dancer, and the shots are coming off your racquet like Nadal's. You could win this match with a broom. Why not also get some extra practice.

* Concentrate on placement of your first serve. Maybe even serve to your opponent's strong side.

* Position yourself to receive serve on your weaker side. Do this just for practice and to build some confidence.

* Instead of just crushing this opponent, try to wear them down. You can hit more shots and get more exercise.

* Practice a stronger second serve, first.

* Have fun, get some practice, but be a little careful in your assessment of the mismatch.

## IF YOU CAN'T WIN, LOSE SMART

Your opponent is more experienced and simply playing on a much higher level. You're having one of those days when your mind is working like glue, your feet are moving like you're wearing weighted boots, and the shots are coming off the racquet like oatmeal. Your opponent is better anyway.

You're going to lose but you still have some choices and some goals you can achieve even though you're on the short end of a mismatch.

* Don't choose to lose "dumb and quick" by trying to hit winners and shots beyond your capabilities.

* Decide to lose smart, by making your opponent WIN every point. Do this by limiting unforced or stupid mental errors.

* Try figuring out why your opponent is so much more effective. What might you learn from this opponent?

* Form some realistic goals within the match. Promise to move your feet more, return every second serve, make your opponent hit three shots every point.

* Decide you are going to stay out on the court as long as you can, even if you're going to lose.

The point here is that no matter what the situation in any given match, you can probably extract a bit more practice or exercise or fun from the experience.

You always have choices, and it is all practice anyway.

# COACH, TALK TO ME!

**"Coach, I always lose to this turkey, and I know I should beat him."**

First forget "should" and figure out "how" to beat him. Figure out why you have lost in the past and plan how to win in the future.

**"Coach, talk about the iron elbow. I can barely breathe on big points. I tighten up like a drum. What can I do?"**

Laughing helps. You can also remind yourself it is all practice. And just practice being loose on these points. Think about it. How important are these points, really?

**"Coach, you say 'don't try for winners.' Don't you have to sometimes in a close match?"**

Sure. But your winner opportunities should be the result of combinations of shots, and they should still be high-percentage shots.

**"Coach, you say we should talk more as a doubles team, but my partner's talking bothers me when I'm about to hit the ball."**

The talking shouldn't be when you're about to hit the ball. You should be talking before the ball is on your side of the net.

# AN OLD PRO'S WISHES

*A long-time teaching pro was finally retiring after many years. This old pro was asked: "You've taught all ages and all abilities. What are your hopes and wishes for your many, many students regarding this game of tennis?"*

*His answer went something like this:*

**I hope they play tennis to win . . .**

**but keep winning in its proper perspective . . .**

**and remember that winning isn't everything, or the only thing, or sometimes even the most important thing . . . .**

**I would want them to remember that winning matches is accomplished by controlling points . . .**

**and that they should not be too reckless or too careful or too serious or too silly on the court . . .**

**that they might laugh as genuinely and easily at their silliest errors and most brilliant winners.**

**I would hope they would always be patient with partners and opponents and with themselves.**

**I hope each one would gain a great deal of joy from this game of tennis and be able to give something back to this great game.**

# PLAYING THE ANGLES

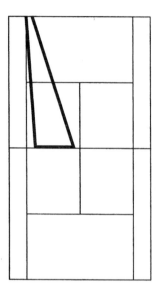

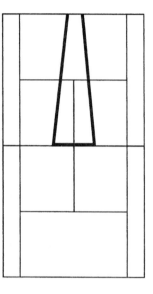

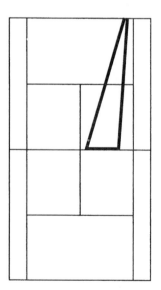

The three court diagrams on this page indicate where a well-hit ground stroke will generally pass over the net when it is hit from the left, the center, and the right.

You never have to cover the entire net. If you can effectively cover the areas of the net indicated in the diagrams, you will hit more winning volleys and force more errors from your opponents.

# PLAYING THE ANGLES

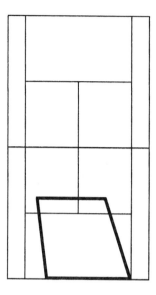

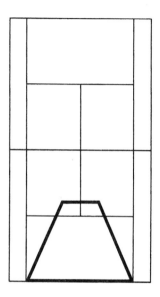

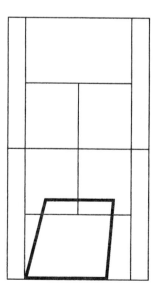

The court diagrams on this page indicate where a well-hit ground stroke will often bounce after it reaches your side of the court when hit from the left, the middle, and the right.

You need not cover the entire court on any given shot. Knowing where a ball will go over the net and where it will bounce can help you tremendously with your positioning and anticipation skills.

# COACH, LOOKS LIKE MY LAST CHANCE

"Coach, I've been using your book and some others and I've been playing tennis, tennis, tennis. I'm exhausted."

Take a break. Play some golf. Take a swim. Go fishing. Stop playing, eating, and sleeping tennis. Give it a rest.

"Coach, you say when I'm playing a weaker player I can hit to their strength and work on my weaknesses. I did this and lost two matches I could have won!"

Sorry. You should only try this if it is a huge mismatch. If you are just a little better than the opponent, this is not a good idea. I owe you one.

"Coach, I can hit that kick serve effectively and consistently in practice, but in a match too many of them fly long."

Your serve is flying long in the match because you've tightened up. In order to get that top spin to bring the ball down in the court, you have to stay loose. Spaghetti arm.

"Coach, I've been trying a lot of stuff in this book and some of it really works. I think I'm playing tennis at a different level now. Amazing."

Thanks, that was the whole idea of the book: to help real players improve their tennis games. I'm glad it worked.

# THE LAST WORD

*Okay. You made it to the last page in the book...and it just seems like way too much stuff to think about. That's all right. Forget about all this stuff and divide your next tennis-playing month into four weeks. Each of these weeks concentrate on the single concept outlined below. That's it. Not a lot of stuff. In a month you'll be playing much better tennis.*

**WEEK #1. Look at the ball.** REALLY concentrate visually on the ball. Look for the seams, the writing, use a bi-colored ball. Watch it come off your opponent's racquet. Do whatever it takes to get you to really watch the ball. Forget about everything else. Put yourself in a Ball-Watching Trance.

**WEEK #2. Move your feet.** Really move your feet. Start moving before the ball is in play. Keep moving until the ball is dead. Stay up on the balls of your feet. Quick, quick, quick small steps, then smoother, longer steps into the shot.

**WEEK #3. Prepare earlier.** Now that you're watching the ball and moving better, you can turn and take your racquet back sooner. Move to the ball with your racquet already back. Anticipate and prepare earlier so you are never rushing your shot. Early. Early. Early.

**WEEK #4. Get your first serve over the net 100% of the time.** Do whatever it takes to get your first serve in the service box AT LEAST 70% of the time. Take off some pace, add some spin, slow down the service motion, whatever you have to do. Get that first serve in the box.

*Please, please don't explain you already do all these things. You may think you are doing them, but you can always do each one much, much better.*

# INDEX

# ABOUT THE AUTHOR

From Connecticut and New York City to Florida and the Caribbean, Dick Myers has been coaching and teaching tennis at every level for over thirty years.

He has coached national champions and has shared the court and his tennis expertise with the "rich and famous" from the worlds of entertainment and business and politics.

He has hosted dozens of world-class tennis talents — Guillermo Vilas, Martina Navratilova, Billie Jean King, Stefan Edberg, Mats Wilander and dozens more — who practiced and played at The Tennis Club, Grand Central Terminal where he was Tennis Director for ten years.

But Mr. Myers's favorite tennis activity, the one he enjoys most, is teaching and working with "regular humans." He believes the recreational player — the weekday and weekend warrior — is what the game of tennis is all about.

Dick lives with his wife, Pam, in Florida and in the Caribbean. Together they have written, edited, and authored over seventy books.